DATE DUE			

Frederic Chopin

FREDERIC CHOPIN

BY VICTOR SEROFF

THE MACMILLAN COMPANY
NEW YORK

Text copyright © Victor Seroff 1964

All Rights Reserved

Library of Congress catalog card number: 64–20733

First Printing

The Macmillan Company, New York
Collier-Macmillan Canada, Ltd., Toronto, Ontario

Designed by Mina Baylis

Printed in the United States of America

TO MY FRIENDS
Edith and Karl Margraf

Foreword

THERE ARE many biographies of Chopin in many languages, but to my knowledge Victor Seroff's is the most concise and readable. The book is especially valuable for the emphasis it places on the composer's love of his country. Chopin, truly the Poet Laureate of Poland, was a man who, for reasons of patriotic pride, exiled himself from his homeland and consequently from the family he loved dearly. This self-imposed exile and the motive behind it account for much of the drama of his life, which Mr. Seroff paints most feelingly.

As a musician, I was intrigued with the chapter in which Chopin gives a piano lesson to his friend Countess Delphine Potočka. Here one is given a glimpse of the composer's attitude to music and to the piano, an instrument he understood with such sensitivity, and whose possibilities he so greatly enlarged.

The Countess, to whom Chopin gave this fascinating lesson, is an important figure in this book. Unlike many of Chopin's biographers, Mr. Seroff is convinced that the great love of the composer's life was not the celebrated lady novelist George

Sand, but the beautiful Potočka, who shared with him a Polish heritage and a love of music.

Victor Seroff is unique in my experience. He is not only a profoundly devoted musical scholar and a brilliant pianist, but also has great literary gifts. All these qualities have made possible this simple but delightful book about Chopin.

LEOPOLD STOKOWSKI

PART ONE
1810~1830

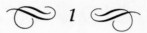

*F*REDERIC CHOPIN is not well known to everyone, even every musician. Singers, wind- and string-instrument players and most performers of popular music may recognize his name, but they have only the vaguest idea of what kind of musician he was. And why should they? Chopin composed almost exclusively for the piano.

For pianists, however, whether students or professionals, Chopin remains an idol. His works are the most beautiful written for the instrument, and as long as the piano exists they will be played and enjoyed as they have been all over the world for more than one hundred years. It is surprising that all pianists, at least, do not know more about Chopin the man.

First, what was his nationality? Chopin is a French name, but he was a Pole. Yet, though he was a Pole, he did not live in the country of his birth but in France. He spoke French but with a foreign accent, because his mother tongue was Polish. And when he died, his heart was cut out and taken to Poland, where it was placed among the other relics at the Church of the Holy Cross in Warsaw, while his body was buried at Père-Lachaise Cemetery in Paris. As his coffin was lowered into the grave, a handful of Polish soil was sprinkled over it.

Would this not confuse anyone unfamiliar with his story?

He inherited his name from his father, Nicolas Chopin, who was a Frenchman. Nicolas was born on April 5, 1771, in Marainville, a small village in Lorraine. He was the son of a wheelwright and wine grower. Whether it was because he did not get along with his family, or because of the intriguing stories he heard about their native country from Poles living in Lorraine, Nicolas migrated to Poland as soon as he was graduated from high school.

At seventeen, he must have been a romantic soul and a brave young man, for he brought nothing except his violin and flute to the strange country where he was going to seek his fortune. At first he tried his hand at several jobs, but finally took a position as a bookkeeper in a snuff factory owned by a Frenchman. (After the Revolution of 1789 in France many Frenchmen emigrated to Poland.)

At the time when Nicolas arrived in Warsaw, Poland was going through one of the many political crises which have beset it throughout its history. No sooner had the Polish King Stanislas Poniatowski agreed to some reforms than the Russians sent their troops against him, and Nicolas saw fighting in the streets.

After the Russians occupied Warsaw, many Polish industries were closed, among them the snuff factory. Left without a job, Nicolas was thinking of returning home to France. After six years this decision was a hard one, but he fell ill before he could leave, and by the time he recovered the Poles were in the midst of rebellion against the Russians. Nicolas already felt so much in sympathy with their cause that he joined the Polish patriots.

He became an officer, and only by chance escaped death.

Had his regiment not moved to another position on the battlefield, he would have been among those massacred by the Russian troops. Again he thought of going back to France, and again he fell ill. This time he decided it must have been his fate to remain in Poland. He never returned to France, not even for a short visit. Eventually he lost touch with his family and most probably never spoke of them, for when his son came to live in Paris he never knew that he had two aunts still living in France.

His decision made, Nicolas had to find some way of earning his living, and this time he turned to an asset that so many Frenchmen in Poland have put to good use. This asset was his knowledge of the French language. The wealthy Poles were eager to engage Frenchmen as teachers to their children, and Nicolas succeeded in obtaining a position as a tutor with the well-to-do Skarbek family.

The Skarbeks, like so many other families of the Polish nobility, owned a large estate in the country. Theirs was at Zelazowa Wola, a village some thirty miles west of Warsaw. Count Skarbek, the head of the family, seems to have preferred to live abroad and enjoy life free from the cares of the estate and his personal responsibilities. These problems and their five children he left with the Countess, his wife. Fortunately, the Countess found an able assistant in a distant relative, Justina Krzyzanowska, an orphan who lived with her.

Justina was twenty years old, blue-eyed, pretty, with delicate features, and a mass of blond hair that she tied in a knot on the top of her head. Always in good humor, she was adored by the whole family, who called her "the court housekeeper," for it was her duty to take care of the house and to look after the growing children.

This is the situation Nicolas found at the Skarbeks when he arrived at Zelazowa Wola in the fall of 1802.

Life on these estates away from the city was rather monot-

JUSTINA AND NICOLAS CHOPIN
(*Pencil sketch by Ambroise Miroszewski*)

onous. After the daily chores were completed, there was nothing to do in the long evenings except chat by the fireside, occasionally with a visitor from the neighborhood, or read old magazines and books. The Skarbeks were delighted, therefore, when they discovered that the newcomer played the violin and the flute. Justina played the piano and had a pleasant soprano voice, and before long the gloomy living room of the manor house was transformed into a joyful meeting place for the family, where they made music, sang, and danced.

In this way four years passed, while Nicolas became more and more like one of the family. Besides tutoring the children and entertaining them as a musician, he helped the Countess with her bookkeeping. His experience at the snuff factory had not been in vain. And, since he had learned a little about medicine in the army, he was also of use to Justina on her errands in the village where she was often called to attend sick peasants.

Small wonder that the two young people grew close together. They fell in love and were married. Nicolas was thirty-five and Justina twenty-four. Thus, Chopin, the composer, had a Polish mother and a French father, who had become Polish by choice.

Chopin was born on February 22, 1810, in a small cottage of three rooms on the Zelazowa Wola estate to which his parents moved after their wedding. He was given two names: Frederic, after Frederic Skarbek who was away; and François, after François Grebecki, who represented the absent Skarbek at the christening.

// There is a story connected with his birth, which may be true or which may have been concocted merely for the benefit of biographers of famous musicians. According to an old custom in the Poland of those days, whenever there was a wedding in a village the peasants, dressed up in their best for the occasion, would come to the manor house playing various instruments, singing and dancing for their landlords. Because there was a wedding on the day of his birth, Chopin may have come into the world accompanied by the strains of music.//

Curiously enough, there is a similar story in connection with the birth of Michael Glinka, one of the great Russian composers of the last century. He was born on his parents' estate six years before Chopin. It is said that at the time of his birth—dawn—a nightingale sang under the window of the room where Michael was born. "Michael is doomed to be a buffoon," his father is supposed to have said, for this Russian nobleman would have considered as an insult the mere suggestion that his son would become a musician. For a nobleman and a wealthy landlord music was a pastime, not an occupation.

It was different in the Chopin family. Theirs was a different attitude toward music and musicians.

*F*REDERIC was the Chopins' second child. Ludwika, his
sister, was three years older. Now, with two children in his
family, Nicolas had to find some other way of earning enough
money to meet expenses. It happened that an instructor in the
lower grades at the French Lyceum in Warsaw fell ill, and the
position was offered to Nicolas. He accepted the appointment,
and the Chopins moved to the quarters reserved for teachers.
In the following years Justina bore two more girls, Emilia and
Isabella. Nicolas, to increase his modest income, not only took
on two more teaching jobs at a military preparatory school and
in a school of artillery and engineering, but obtained permission from the Lyceum authorities to take in boarders—school-
boys whose homework he supervised. Then, more or less free
of financial problems, Nicolas, Justina, and the children could
devote themselves to their home, and to music.

Ludwika, the most robust of the children, was very helpful
to her parents at an early age. She was endowed with intelligence and some musical talent. From her parents she learned
to read and write both Polish and French, and from her mother
to play the piano. She was the ringleader in all the games with

Above: LUDWIKA CHOPIN
Above, right: ISABELLA CHOPIN
Below: EMILIA CHOPIN

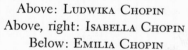

her brother and sisters. And, as if it were just another game, she herself taught Frederic to read and write Polish and French. But Frederic was more fascinated with the music she or their mother played, and he used to crawl under the piano and sit and listen there quietly. Often, they said, they would find him there crying; this, they thought, was not caused by pain but

rather by pure enjoyment. Sometimes, later on, he would stand
by Ludwika or his mother's side while they played the piano
and would watch their hands moving over the keyboard. Then
he, too, would try to strike the keys and would listen to the
sounds his little fingers managed to produce.

//According to one story told by the family, everybody was
awakened one night by their maid crying that there was a
ghost in the house. They discovered that it was Frederic in
his nightshirt trying to pick out on the keyboard the melodies
he had heard his mother play. Ludwika determined to start
teaching him to play the piano. Considering his age—he was
barely five years old—Frederic showed an extraordinary ability
to grasp and execute everything Ludwika showed him. And
within a year he had made such progress that it became obvious
he needed a more experienced teacher than his nine-year-old
sister. Nicolas thereupon asked Adalbert Zywny to take charge
of his boy's musical education.

Zywny was quite a character, the kind you are apt to see in
the operas of Mozart or Rossini wearing an old-fashioned wig,
knee breeches, and white stockings. Zywny was a tall man, and
usually dressed in a long green frock coat. He wore a large
white cravat and a yellow velvet vest, and neither in winter nor
in summer did he part with his high black knee-length boots.
The children wondered whether he slept in them. Zywny was
sixty years old, with lively little blue eyes and a goatee, which
like the rest of his weird outfit he tried vainly to free from
bits of tobacco. He was constantly taking snuff and wiping
his long nose with a large red checkered handkerchief, which
otherwise hung loosely out of his coat pocket. His nose was
unusually red, a condition attributed to his fondness for
liquor—vodka in particular.

Zywny, a Czech, had studied music in Vienna, and had been
brought to Poland by a Polish prince who appointed him one
of his "court musicians." But when the prince lost his estate,

ADALBERT ZYWNY

Zywny lost his post and came to Warsaw to seek his livelihood as a piano teacher. Not one of the best teachers in the city, he nevertheless managed to earn enough money from his private pupils to satisfy his modest needs. But he was disillusioned with the work and had long given up his dream of discovering a great talent among his pupils. It is easy to understand with what joy and newly awakened enthusiasm he began to teach Frederic, who was then a little over six years old. At last, he thought, he had a pupil with whom he could share his knowledge.

Frederic was a frail little boy. His delicate face with its high forehead, thin nose, and whimsical gray eyes was framed by blond hair, which fell in waves down to his shoulders. He was not a good-looking boy, but Zywny, after playing for Frederic, saw before him the face of an inspired being carried away into his own dream-world.

Zywny may have smelled of snuff, or—even worse—of vodka, and he may have used his large pencil on his pupils' fingers more often than was necessary, but beneath his eccentricities there was a true musician's nature devoted to art. He could recognize a beautiful composition when he heard it and a true talent when he saw it.

Many a teacher has died forgotten or even unrecognized, because poverty and his own problems kept him from leaving behind any traces of his talents. But not so with Zywny. Instinctively Frederic was drawn to him and followed his advice. Zywny taught him to love Bach and Mozart's compositions, and when much later Frederic became a great pianist he always remained grateful to his funny old teacher. When he was asked where he had learned to play so well, he invariably answered: "Who wouldn't learn to play the piano from a man like Zywny!"

His lessons with Zywny soon became irregular, but not to Frederic's disadvantage. Zywny used to spend all his free time at Chopin's home, coming there for a game of cards, or a long evening by the fireside when he delighted them with stories about the musicians he used to know in Vienna. At the time, Vienna was the world center of musical life. We can be sure that Zywny often illustrated his stories at the piano and that many problems of technique which intrigued Frederic were dealt with at these improvised sessions.

It was to Zywny that Frederic confided his secret desire to compose his own music, and it was Zywny who wrote out Frederic's early attempts. Frederic's phenomenal musical memory made it possible for him to remember his own improvisations and play them over and over again until Zywny could write them down. These early compositions were marches and polonaises: the polonaise is a majestic Polish dance to which later, as a mature composer, Frederic gave superb refinement.

As was to be expected, Zywny was bubbling with pride, and everywhere he went he talked about the accomplishments of his pupil. Not only did all Chopin's neighbors hear about it, but soon Zywny began taking Frederic to perform at the homes of wealthy and noble Poles in Warsaw. Finally the rumor of his extraordinary talent reached Grand Duke Constantine, the Czar's viceroy, who represented the Imperial Russian Government.

Frederic, who was then eight years old, was summoned to the Palace. After he had played, among other pieces, a march of his own, the Grand Duke asked him in his gruff manner, "Why are you looking upward? Do you read your music on the ceiling?" Obviously Frederic was playing everything by heart.

The Grand Duke liked the march so much that he made him play it over and over again, and then he ordered the piece to be orchestrated and played at parades. Although this composition was never published, Frederic often heard it played by military bands.

But Zywny saw to it that at least one of Frederic's polonaises was published. Zywny's friend, the Reverend Cibulski, who often heard Frederic play, had a printing shop in his parish, and one day Zywny proudly presented the Chopins with their son's first engraved composition. Shortly afterward the Warsaw magazine *Review*, in an article entitled "List of Polish Works Published in 1817," not only mentioned this composition but also praised the prodigious pianistic talent of the young composer. This was Frederic's first introduction as a musician to the public at large.

Contrary to what happened in other families, the Chopins never thought to exploit their son's unusual talent financially. Needless to say, they were very proud of his success, yet they realized that he still had before him years of study both in music and general education. They would not let this initial success turn their heads. Frederic was to continue his classes at the Lyceum and play with his schoolmates as any other growing boy.

"The Young Chopin" (*Painting by Gow*)

And what about Frederic? Did it turn his head? How did he feel about being treated as a prodigy and compared to Mozart? The boy was truly modest and did not seem to be affected by all the praise he heard at the homes of the aristocrats, all those princes and princesses, counts and countesses; nor by the fact that after he performed for the Grand Duke, a carriage was often sent to take him to the Palace to play with the Grand Duke's children; nor by the fact that he stole the show at a concert on February 24, 1818—his first public appearance.

After long deliberation his parents consented to his participation in a benefit performance organized by the leading families of Warsaw society. There were several artists on the program, but Frederic's performance of Adalbert Gyrovetz's *Piano Concerto* created a sensation.

After the concert, Zywny and Nicolas reported every detail of the event to Justina, who could not attend it because of an illness. They told her over and over again how he looked in his dark velvet jacket, short trousers, and white stockings, how he took a bow, how he played, and about the wild enthusiasm of the audience.

"But Frederic," Justina asked, "tell me! What did they like best?"

"The white collar you gave me to wear," was all that Frederic replied.

Perhaps it was he himself who liked the white collar best. Already in his childhood he was attracted by beautiful clothes, and all his life he paid special attention to his wardrobe. Like most children, Frederic was too young to be handicapped by a sense of responsibility; at the concert he played just as well as if he were playing alone for himself. Later, the more famous he became the less Frederic liked to play in public, and did so only out of pure financial necessity.

3

*F*OUR years passed, during which Frederic made remarkable progress in his piano playing. On April 23, 1821, for Zywny's birthday, Frederic presented him with a polonaise, which he dedicated to him. The old man was very much touched—he was proud of Frederic—but he was also very sad. It somehow struck him as a symbolic gesture from a grateful pupil who no longer needed his teacher.

For some time Zywny had been overwhelmed by Frederic's accomplishments, and he felt that the boy already knew as much as he could teach him. Zywny could merely console himself by saying: "I would have been a poor teacher indeed if my pupils didn't surpass me."

But he remained Frederic's faithful friend, and for the rest of his life he was always welcome at the Chopin home to share the family's joys and sorrows, to join them in their games of cards, or to spend an evening by the fireside. Zywny continued to follow Frederic's musical career, was always present wherever he was invited to play, took him to concerts and the opera, and introduced him to all the visiting celebrities, including Angelica Catalani, the famous singer. After hearing Frederic play, she presented him with a gold watch which he treasured the rest of his life.

Thus it was only their piano lessons that came to an end. What Frederic needed now was a serious study of composition. Zywny recommended Joseph Elsner, the director of the Warsaw Opera and a composer who was greatly esteemed in the city. But before we speak of another teacher who contributed to Frederic's musicianship, let us take a look at what he was doing when not at his studies.

During those four years Nicolas' financial situation improved. He had been promoted to a higher position at the Lyceum, and was teaching French language and literature in the upper grades. He received a better salary, and the family moved to larger quarters, where they had as many as eight boarders, Frederic's schoolmates.

When people said that "Frederic was growing up like the other boys," what they meant was that besides going to school he played games with them, either in public parks or at home. But that was not Frederic's only recreation. Always in good humor, Frederic was witty and even mischievous. He was good at drawing and had an observant eye for drawing caricatures and a talent for impersonating those whose mannerisms amused him. Most probably Frederic could have become a good actor, but music was his chief interest.

He passed the examinations and was admitted to the fourth grade at the Lyceum; on the whole, he was considered a good student. He excelled in Polish literature and history, but mathematics, natural science, and Latin and Greek bored him, and he was often caught drawing caricatures in his copybooks while the teacher was lecturing. His pranks, however, were overlooked by the school authorities, for they were very proud to have enrolled a talented boy who won favors at the homes of Warsaw society, and about whom there were notices written in the newspapers.

Two crayon caricatures by Frederic Chopin

Frederic's schoolmates liked him because, despite his priv- <inline-note>◡ ॽ/</inline-note>
ileged position among them, he was not a show-off. He was
always ready to join them in their practical jokes and mischief.
And it was the same at home, where after school hours he was
part of a whole community: the eight boarders and his sisters.

Ludwika, once the ringleader in their games, now had to
relinquish her position in favor of her brother. A talented
child, she played the piano and composed, but not as well as
Frederic, and though she wrote poems her literary ability was
not equal to that of her younger sister Emilia.

Frail, and often an invalid, the ten-year-old Emilia was an
intelligent and very imaginative little girl. She seemed to have
a limitless supply of ideas for *tableaux vivants*, which were
very popular in those days. *Tableaux vivants* were staged in

theaters and also at home, and everyone—including the children—loved to participate in them. For a given idea the performers would dress themselves up to represent one or another character in the motionless "picture." And unless Frederic had a role in it, he would provide the appropriate improvised accompaniment on the piano.

These dignified performances, however, could not exhaust the exuberant energies of the boys. They needed more action and more noise. With solemn faces they listened obediently to Frederic's "serious" playing on the piano, but they preferred the "little Mozart" to join them in "taking off" their teachers or the grown ups whom otherwise they did not dare criticize.

Frederic and Emilia also started what they called a "Literary Entertainment Society." He was the president and Emilia the secretary of this club, while everybody else was invited to be a member. They issued their own newspaper and wrote short plays, which the boys and girls had to perform.

Frederic spent his summer vacations from the Lyceum in the country: the first at the Skarbeks' estate, which he had not seen since he was born, the following two at an estate belonging to the family of one of his schoolmates, and the last at a health resort to which his mother took him.

Perhaps because of the stories about Poland he heard from his father, or the lessons in Polish literature and history he enjoyed at school, Frederic even at this early age became a patriot. Out of the city for the first time, he savored his country, began to love its hilly landscape, its forests, ponds, and orchards, the grass in the fields, and the very smell of the air. The sounds he heard while walking in the woods, the singing of the birds, and songs and dances of the peasants in the village—all these were Polish, all a part of his country, which, he believed, should be expressed in his compositions. Now he understood what Zywny used to tell him, that music should have a national character.

On evenings when they did not stage the *tableaux*, the piano under which Frederic as a child first heard the sounds of music was brought out into the garden and placed beneath the elm trees, so that he could play for the family and the neighbors who came to visit them. The hospitable Skarbeks made the Chopins' stay extremely pleasant, but their happiness was marred by anxiety over Frederic's health. He was so pale, his body so frail. Nicolas consulted doctors, and for his second summer vacation Frederic was sent to Szafarino, an estate owned by the Dzievanovskis, the parents of Dominik, Frederic's schoolmate.

The summer at Szafarino was the first time he had been away from his family, and he was homesick. He loved his parents and his sisters, and he missed them. So Frederic kept a diary in which he tried to share everything, no matter how trivial, with his family, as if he never had left them. This diary he called the *Szafarino Courier*, and he was its editor and sole contributor under the pen name "Pichon"—obviously derived from his own name, Chopin.

The Dzievanovskis were very thoughtful and tried to make him as happy as they could. They took him on long rides to see the country and the neighboring villages, where they stopped at old inns to watch peasants singing and dancing.

It was at Szafarino that Frederic had his first lessons in horseback riding and shooting, so that on his second visit, the following summer, he was good enough to take part in hunting and returned home with two birds and a hare dangling from his belt.

Frederic also enjoyed his stay with the Dzievanovskis because, in the evenings, he could play duets either with Madame Dzievanovska or one of her daughters, and because in them he found an appreciative audience for the few short pieces he happened to compose there. Among these was a *Mazurka in A minor*, the prototype of the one later published among his

works as Opus 17, Number 4. Most probably it was inspired
by a song and a dance he saw at an inn in the village.

Frederic's parents, however, did not send him to Szafarino
to compose, but rather to have fresh air and good rest, to
take long walks, and, above all, to observe a strict diet. Justina gave all necessary instructions to Madame Dzievanovska,
and Frederic kept strictly to it. He took the pills his mother
gave him to gain weight, drank half a bottle of linden infusion
and six glasses of roasted acorn coffee each day, and ate white
rolls baked specially for him.

Whether this curious diet did him much good is question-
able. The boy was definitely threatened by tuberculosis, and
while the fresh country air and exercise gave him an outwardly
improved appearance, there was no concealing the fact that
whenever he joined his friends in dancing he soon had to stop
for lack of breath. His parents let him go through another
school year at the Lyceum, but on the day after his final
examinations he had to be taken, on doctors' orders, to
Reinerz, a health resort in Silesia.

This time he did not go alone. Justina went along with his
two sisters: Emilia, who was suffering from the same illness,
though her case was even further advanced than Frederic's;
and Ludwika, who came to help her mother. For five weeks at
Reinerz Frederic had to submit to the rigorous daily routine
of the spa, which he described in a letter to a friend:

I have been drinking whey and the local waters and they say
that I look better. I am told that I am getting fat, and am as lazy
as ever. In the morning, by six o'clock at the latest, all the patients
are at the wells where there is an atrocious band of wind players—
a dozen freaks of various types gathered together. The principal
player, a gaunt bassoonist with a snuffy, spectacled nose, frightens
all the ladies. Then there is a sort of parade or masquerade, but not
everyone is masked. This promenade along the beautiful avenues
that connect the establishment with the town usually lasts until

REINERZ. At right is theater in which Chopin gave two concerts.

eight, or according to the number of glasses a person has to drink in the morning. Then everyone goes home for breakfast. After breakfast people usually go for a walk. I walk until twelve; then eat dinner, because after dinner one has to go to the well. After dinner there is usually a bigger parade than in the morning, because everyone is dressed up, all in different clothes from those of the morning. Again there is the vile music and so it goes until evening. . . . After supper I go to bed. So . . . do I have time for writing letters? It is true that when I walk on the hills that encircle Reinerz, I am often so delighted with the view of these valleys that I hate to come down. I have not yet been on the excursion that everyone takes, for it is forbidden me. Near Reinerz there is a mountain with a wonderful view, but the air at the very top is not good for everybody, and unfortunately I am one of the patients to whom it is not allowed.

As for the ways of the place, I am so used to them that nothing bothers me. At first it seemed strange to me that the women work more than the men, but as I don't do anything, myself, it is easy for me to accept it. There have been many Poles in Reinerz, nearly all were acquaintances of mine, but now the company is thinning. . . . I must go to the well now for my two glasses of water and a piece of gingerbread.

Above all, Frederic missed having a good piano. Still, when he heard about an accident which left several children orphans and penniless, Frederic, with Justina and Ludwika's help, organized a benefit performance at which he played. It was so successful that it had to be repeated. These were his first recitals in a foreign country.

By now it was obvious that Frederic was destined to have a professional musical career. His parents decided that his studies under Elsner were far more important than regular school classes and that he should not return to the Lyceum.

His health may have improved, but Emilia's did not. Upon their return home she steadily grew weaker. "Horrors, horrors," Frederic wrote to Titus Voyciechovski, his most intimate friend. "All this time she has eaten nothing. She has grown so thin you wouldn't recognize her." A month later, on April 10, 1827, the fourteen-year-old Emilia died of tuberculosis of the lungs. It was a terrible blow to the Chopin family. Her death heightened anxiety about Frederic's health.

Impatient to begin his work with Elsner, Frederic readily agreed with his parents' decision about the Lyceum. "Really it would be stupid to sit still for six hours a day," he reasoned, "when both German and German-Polish doctors have ordered me to walk as much as I can. It would be silly to listen to the same things over and over when one could be learning something new." Instead, he took some courses at the University "on subjects in any way touching on music," as he said. These were lectures on literature and history. To his knowledge of the Polish, French, and German languages he added a study of Italian.

❦ 4 ❦

Joseph Elsner, the only other music teacher Frederic ever had, differed considerably from Zywny. For no apparent reason and with no possible hope of profit Elsner had concocted a romantic story of his background, which eventually he believed himself. He claimed that he was of Swedish origin, a descendant of the royal Vasas, and that one of his supposed ancestors came to Poland and married "a beautiful Polish girl." He did not bestow a title upon himself, but to bear out his masquerade he used a seal representing a knight leaning on two shields; on one of them was engraved a bull's head surmounted by a plume and a five-pointed coronet; on the other was his monogram, "J.E."

Actually Elsner was a German, born in Silesia. His father, a manufacturer of musical instruments, sent him to Wroclaw, Poland, to become a clergyman. But because he would have had to learn the Polish language—something he did not want to do—he shifted from theological studies to medicine and music. His skill with the violin gave him an opportunity to start on a professional career as a musician. After one year as a first violinist in a theater orchestra in Brno, today in Czecho-

slovakia, he returned to Poland where he became a conductor at the opera at Lwow. During his stay there he lost his aversion to the sound of the Polish language, perhaps because he remembered he had Polish as well as royal Swedish blood in his veins. In Lwow, Elsner composed five operas, all using Polish liberettos. A prolific man, he wrote some twenty-seven operas, Masses and choral works, as well as mazurkas and waltzes, which became very popular all over Poland.

Elsner stayed seven years in Lwow before coming to Warsaw to take a position as a director of the Opera and a teacher of composition at the Conservatory. There Frederic entered Elsner's class, in which he was to receive a thorough knowledge of theoretical subjects: seven hours a week were devoted to harmony, counterpoint, and composition, as well as six hours to practical exercise. Although Elsner strictly followed the prescribed programs in these studies, which also included exercises in orchestration, Frederic submitted only reluctantly to this discipline. He lagged behind his classmates, and brought Elsner only mazurkas, polonaises, and waltzes for approval. Because of their originality, Elsner did not reprimand Frederic, but made him an exception and guided him in his endeavor. It was no use trying to force the young man to write vocal or orchestral music; he insisted that these did not inspire him. He was entirely preoccupied with one instrument—the piano.

During the following three years at the Conservatory, until he was eighteen, Frederic worked hard at his own compositions, several of which were published later on: *Rondo in F major à la Mazur* (Opus 5), *Polonaise in D minor* (Opus 71, Number 1), and the *Mazurka in A minor* (Opus 68, Number 2). He heard a great deal of music, not only at the Conservatory but at concerts and operas that he attended, and at Elsner's home, where the director's pupils met to play for one another their own compositions and other works they had "discovered."

Frederic was so impressed by John Field's nocturnes, for instance, that he, too, composed in this until then unknown musical form. His first *Nocturne* (Opus 72, Number 1) remained unpublished until after his death, because having later perfected the nocturne, he was never satisfied with his early attempt. Also, most probably to please Elsner, Frederic wrote *Variations for piano and orchestra on "Là ci darem la mano"* from Mozart's opera *Don Giovanni*. This was his first composition for piano and orchestra. With it perhaps he proved what he had been saying to Elsner all along, that he did not feel secure in writing for an orchestra. Still, the work was eventually published as Opus 2.

Despite his hard work Frederic continued to lead a busy social life. His company was very much in demand. Warsaw society figures and aristocrats vied with each other to have him at their homes, not only as composer but as an actor to take part in some of their theatrical performances. But both Justina and Nicolas now felt that his popularity in Warsaw or even Poland alone was not sufficient; he needed broader recognition, new contacts. Such an opportunity was offered by

Felix Jarotski, Professor of Natural History at the University
of Warsaw. He was an old friend of Nicolas, and he suggested taking Frederic to Berlin, where he had been invited
to attend an international congress of naturalists.

Frederic was very excited about the trip. Besides the chance
of seeing another country and hearing new music, he hoped
to meet Spontini, Mendelssohn, and at least hear Paganini,
whose triumphal concert tour through Germany had been
sweeping audiences off their feet. Jarotski and the Polish Prince
Antoni Radziwill were to introduce him to "people." The
Prince, besides being a very rich and influential man, was a
great lover of music. Frederic had played for him during a
visit to his estate, Antonin, and since the Prince particularly
enjoyed chamber music, Frederic had even started a Trio he
planned to dedicate to him.

Once in Berlin, after a strenuous five-day trip by stagecoach,
Jarotski dragged Frederic to all kinds of sessions connected
with the congress of naturalists. Frederic was thirsting for
music, but managed to hear only two operas, Weber's *Der
Freischütz*, and Spontini's *Cortez*. "I saw Spontini, Zelter, and
Mendelssohn," he wrote home, "but I did not speak with any
of them, because I was too timid to introduce myself."

Prince Radziwill did not come to Berlin, nor did Paganini.
Disappointed, with nothing to show for his journey except a
portfolio filled with the caricatures of the prominent naturalists he drew while bored at the congress, Frederic urged Jarotski
to return to Warsaw. On their way home, at a small post
station, they were told that there were no fresh horses available
and they would be delayed. Jarotski was satisfied to pass the
time eating and drinking, and Frederic discovered a piano in a
guest room of the inn. It is certain that this old piano had
never before produced such sounds as it did under Frederic's
fingers.

In no time he had a large audience, including the post-

Chopin at the piano, 1826 (*Pencil drawing by Eliza Radziwill*)

master, his wife, and two daughters. When the horses were ready to start out, and Frederic was about to stop playing, his audience would not let him go. They pleaded with him to continue. The postmaster promised to give him his best horses, and his wife served them food and wine just to keep Frederic playing.

It was in this little inn that he improvised the beginning of his future *Grand Fantasy on Polish Airs* (Opus 13). Later on, he remembered this incident, as well as the girls who brought him sweets when he and Jarotski boarded the stagecoach. "One of them was very pretty," Frederic said.

Was she the first pretty girl he had ever noticed? Certainly not. Frederic could not have missed noticing pretty girls at the homes of aristocrats in Warsaw, to which he was invited for parties and dancing. At the age of ten, when Grand Duke Constantine's carriage used to bring him to the Palace, he especially liked playing duets with the pretty ten-year-old Countess Alexandrine de Moriolles. Five years later his classmates teased him about his "first love." They had seen him meeting her in the botanical garden where, in acacia-lined alleys, the students liked to study for their final examinations. At the age of seventeen he dedicated to her, whom he called the "little devil," his *Rondo à la Mazur*.

When they were at Reinerz, both Justina and Ludwika had noticed that Frederic particularly liked the pretty Czech girl Libusha, who waited on the guests at the spring, to which he came twice a day for the prescribed drinking of water. It was Libusha's father, a foundry worker, who was killed in an accident, and it was for her and her sisters' benefit that Frederic gave his two Reinerz concerts.

On his return from Berlin, he began going to the home of Count Wodzinski to teach his daughter Maria the piano. Although Frederic was already eighteen and Maria's three older brothers were about his age, the piano lessons with their sister often ended with all of them engrossed in childish games and pranks, and Frederic running after Maria shouting that he loved her. (Actually he was in love, not with Maria, but with Konstancya Gladkowska, whom he had heard at a concert.

She was a beautiful girl, blonde, with dark blue eyes and a graceful figure. She was not from a wealthy family (her father was one of the superintendents of the royal castle), but she was always dressed with such taste that she was conspicuous even among the women of Warsaw society. Frederic had many occasions to meet her; yet he was content to admire her from afar—in a church or theater. Though at that time he spoke to no one about his feelings, her image did not leave his heart.

At the Conservatory it became apparent that continued study was not going to give Frederic any more knowledge and experience. His "practical exercises" always turned out to be new compositions; he still showed no interest in vocal or orchestral music. Elsner, to whom an opera was the supreme form of composition, urged him in vain to write one. Finally, he had to accept Frederic's "limitations," had to let him develop his art in his own way. Elsner had done his job: he had given Frederic the assurance which every beginner needs; he could do no more.

Thus 1829 was Frederic's last year at the Conservatory. The "practical exercises" had to give way to "experience," which he was to gain from broadening the field of his activities. Elsner, Zywny, the Skarbeks, and his parents all urged him to go to Vienna and try to do there what he had failed to do in Berlin—to make new contacts, to arrange for the publication of his compositions, and perhaps even to try gaining recognition by playing his own works at a concert.

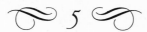

*A*FTER a week of sight-seeing at Cracow, once the capital
of Poland, Frederic, accompanied by four classmates, arrived
in Vienna on the last day of August, 1829. He immediately
called on Wenzel Würfel and Thomas Niedecki, who Frederic's well-wishers in Warsaw hoped would help him in the
strange city. Würfel was a conductor and a famous pianist.
He remembered Frederic well, since Zywny had often taken
him to the Chopins' home to show off his talented pupil, who
was at the time only eight years old. Neidecki, like Frederic,
had been a pupil of Elsner.

Both men were happy to see Frederic, and took delight in
showing him houses and streets where Mozart, Haydn, Beethoven, and Schubert had lived. They also introduced him to
the prominent musicians still active at that time in a city
glorious in its musical history.

Beethoven had died eighteen months before Frederic came
to Vienna, but he met some of those who had known the
composer. It was a great treat for him to hear stories of Czerny,
Beethoven's pupil and in turn Liszt's teacher, whose *Etudes*
every beginning student diligently practices even today; of

Giulietta Guicciardi, to whom Beethoven dedicated his *Moon-light Sonata*; and of Ignaz Schuppanzigh, Beethoven's lifelong friend, who no longer played in public. Würfel took him to see Adalbert Gyrovetz, whose *Concerto* Frederic had played at his first concert at the age of eight, and Tobias Haslinger, the music publisher to whom Zywny had sent Frederic's *Varia-tions on "Là ci darem la mano."* And finally Würfel intro-duced him to Count Wenzel von Gallenberg, the owner of Kärtnertor theater, the largest concert hall in Vienna.

Frederic played at their homes, and they all urged him to give a concert. But Frederic hesitated. He had not practiced the piano for two full weeks—one spent in Cracow, and the other in Vienna making a round of visits. But once Haslinger, who had not yet published the *Variations*, impressed on him the importance of a personal appearance, Frederic consented.

Von Gallenberg offered his hall, and Frederic in turn agreed to play without fee, for, as he reported to his family, the Count's purse was nearly empty. In those days it was unheard of for a pianist to give a recital by himself, so Gallenberg arranged a full program for the concert: first Beethoven's *Prometheus* Overture, to be followed by Frederic playing his own *Variations*; then, after three Rossini arias to be sung by Charlotte Veltheim of the Saxon court opera, Frederic was to play *Concerto Rondo à la Krakowiak* (Opus 14), a work for piano and orchestra completed in 1828. Another vocal number and a short ballet were to round out the performance.

On the night of the recital the hall was not full. It was summer, when many Viennese were away in the country, and Chopin's name was unknown to the public. But the small audience reacted enthusiastically.

"I played with desperation," Frederic said afterward. Never before had he sat alone on the stage while the orchestra was in the pit. And when some of his *Variations* were interrupted by applause he could hardly hear the orchestra.

The Kärtnertor theater in Vienna

At the rehearsal it was discovered that the musicians had trouble reading their parts of his *Concerto Rondo à la Krakowiak*, therefore a so-called "Free Fantasy" had to be substituted. This consisted of Frederic's extempore improvisations on a theme given by the audience, in this case a melody from Boïeldieu's *La Dame blanche,* an opera which he had heard only a few days before. Long years of experience—he had improvised ever since he was a child wherever and whenever he was asked to play in Warsaw—had made him a master of the art. And when he spiced his improvisations with the Polish drinking song "The Hop Plant," the audience was enchanted.

The day after the performance, Frederic wrote a full account to his parents:

Yesterday, that is on Tuesday at seven in the evening, in the Royal Opera House I made my entry into the world! . . . As soon as I appeared on the stage the bravos began; after each *Variation* the applause was so loud that I couldn't hear the orchestra. When I finished they clapped so much that I had to go out to bow a second time. In the "Free Fantasy" the solo improvisations didn't go off quite so well, but there were a lot of clapping and bravos, and I had to go out again. . . . My friends and colleagues spread themselves through the hall to listen to opinions and criticisms. "Too bad the young man is so poorly dressed," one Viennese woman remarked. If that is all the fault anybody found—and otherwise they assure me that they heard only compliments, and that they themselves never started bravos—then I don't have to worry! All the same it is being said everywhere that I played "too softly," or, rather, too delicately, for people are used to the piano-pounding of the artists here. I expect to find this reproach in the paper, especially as the journalist's daughter Leopoldine Blahetka thumps frightfully. It doesn't really matter, there must always be a *but* somewhere, and I would prefer this one to having people say that I played "too loudly."

"Playing softly" was the most characteristic trait of Chopin the pianist, one for which he was criticized whenever he played in public. It did not mean, however, that he played everything *piano*, in a monotonous *mezzo voce*. On the contrary, his playing had a large dynamic range with extraordinary nuances. He simply did not believe in pounding or, as he said, "thumping the keys with crashing chords." Chopin's frailty did not influence the manner of his playing; rather, it stemmed from his regard for the piano as an instrument.

Since the piano cannot reproduce orchestral sounds or even the sounds of individual instruments, but can only imitate or suggest them, Chopin saw no reason to demand more from the instrument than it can give naturally. He felt that the "orchestral" approach favored by the great virtuosos produced more noise than music and was ugly, even painful to his ears. In his own range Chopin employed all the gradations from *pianissimo* to *fortissimo*, but on a smaller, more restricted and better controlled scale of volume.

It would be unfair to say that the music critics failed to appreciate his individual approach. But the general public at the time—as even today, unfortunately—was more impressed by virtuosos who exaggerated both volume and speed in their performances.

Notwithstanding any criticism, Chopin's first concert was such a success that he had to agree to give another. "I shan't give a third concert, and wouldn't even give the second, except they insist on it," he wrote home to his parents. "Besides, it occurred to me that people in Warsaw might say: 'What's this? He gave only one concert and then left? Perhaps it was a failure.' "

But, far from failure, his second concert brought him even more applause then the first. It was attended by the leading musicians in the city, and with deserved pride Frederic reported that "beginning with the conductor and ending with the piano-tuner they were surprised by the beauty of my compositions. I know that both ladies and artists like me"—something that from that time on Chopin could truthfully say for the rest of his life.

The day after his concert he started on the stagecoach journey home. Although he was armed with letters of introduction which would have led to more concerts in Prague and Dresden while on the way back to Warsaw, Frederic preferred to have a vacation. There may have been another reason too: he heard that only shortly before his arrival in Prague, Paganini had given a concert there and was "torn to shreds" by the music critics. Frederic wisely preferred to bring his Viennese laurels home unblemished.

In Prague he visited the Czech National Museum, the amethyst-studded St. Wenceslas Chapel, and the Hradčany, an old castle on a hill with a magnificent view over *Zlata Praha*, "Golden Prague," with all its gilded baroque churches. In Dresden he saw the famous Dresden gallery, and in the evening sat through a performance of Goethe's *Faust* which lasted for five hours. "A terrible but a great fantasy," Frederic called the work. He could not escape several invitations to the country estates of local aristocrats, who in turn gave him letters of introduction to visit their friends. But Frederic had already been two months away from home, the longest time he had ever been separated from his family. He was homesick, and he cut his visits short to speed his return to Warsaw.

∾ 6 ∾

 P EOPLE used to say that Chopin was never happy where he was, that he always wanted to be somewhere else. This must have been true even in his youth. After he was home a few weeks he said to his friend, Titus: "You can't imagine how dreary Warsaw seems to me now; if it were not for my family cheering me up, I shouldn't be able to stay."

Later he wrote a letter to his friend:

You want to know what I intend to do with myself this winter? Well, I won't stay in Warsaw, that much I know. It is true that Prince Radziwill, or rather the Princess, who is very kind, has invited me to Berlin, even asking me to stay at their own palace, but of what use will this be to me now when I should go back to Vienna where I made my debut. . . . You must realize yourself that this is necessary for me but not on account of Mademoiselle Blahetka, about whom, I think, I have written you—she is young, pretty, and a pianist.

Leopoldine Blahetka, whom Frederic had met soon after his arrival in Vienna, was the daughter of an influential journalist and was herself a concert pianist. Frederic played duets with her at her father's home, but he enjoyed her good looks more than her playing. She was like so many other virtuosos he had already heard, "thumping the keyboard." To assure Titus that he would not return to Vienna merely because of Mademoiselle Blahetka, Frederic confided something he had never mentioned to anybody. "Perhaps unfortunately, I have my own ideal. I have served her faithfully (although I have never spoken to her) for half a year; an ideal of whom I dream, to whom the Adagio of my concerto belongs, and who this morning inspired the little Waltz I am sending you. Note one place: *x*. No one knows this except you."

This *Waltz*, published after Chopin's death as Opus 73, Number 3, was erroneously dated 1830; he had written it a year before. A work of charming simplicity, it seems to be a whispered message to the girl he "idealized"; almost as fragile as his feelings were, the piece never rises in volume above *mezzo forte*.

As for the Adagio, he meant the second movement of his F minor *Concerto*. Chopin started this composition in 1828, beginning not with the first, but the second movement, perhaps because of his feelings for Konstancya Gladkowska, his "ideal."

When Frederic returned from Vienna he had ample opportunity to meet and talk with her. Konstancya practiced in the classroom reserved for singers and lived at the Conservatory boardinghouse reserved for scholarship students. But Frederic held back still, expressing his emotions through his compositions. He worked diligently on them in his new room above his parents' apartment, which they had furnished for him, now that he was an independent young man.

At this time, besides his work on the *Concerto*, he composed two *Mazurkas*, another *Waltz*, and, of all things, a *Funeral March*—most probably when he felt despondent over his love. But Frederic grew restless. He decided to pay a visit to Antonin, the Radziwills' estate.

The Radziwills were a very musical family. The Prince

Above:
Chopin playing in the salon
of Prince Radziwill
(*Painting by Siemisadszki*)

Left:
KONSTANCYA GLADKOWSKA

composed, and played the cello while Frederic accompanied
him at the piano. The young Princesses took lessons from
Frederic, and each evening was turned into a regular concert.
The family made Frederic's stay so pleasant that he said he
would never leave unless he were "driven out." But he underestimated the force of his love for Konstancya, sentimental
and innocent though it was. He said it was work left unfinished
in his room—he was still rewriting the last movement of his
F minor *Concerto*—but it was his constant thought of Konstancya that eventually "drove" him back to Warsaw.

In the capital, Frederic gave two recitals for a group of invited guests at his home. The critics reviewed these favorably.
Finally, on March 17, 1830, he gave his first public concert at
the National Theater. He played the F minor *Concerto*, and
after the customary numbers by other artists, closed the
evening by playing the *Grand Fantasy on Polish Airs*.

Frederic may have hoped to impress Konstancya with his
reputation before attempting to introduce himself. However, he was so well praised in the Warsaw press, both as a
composer and a pianist, that, at long last, he had gained enough
self-confidence to speak to her.

Konstancya was not only one of the prettiest girls at the
Conservatory, but she was talented, hard-working, and extremely ambitious: she wanted to become an opera singer.
The many compliments she received for her looks and her
singing gave Konstancya a certain sober self-assurance that one
would not have expected in a woman so young. Konstancya
was twenty, only three months younger than Frederic, but
far more mature than he. Still, Frederic's knowledge of music
was naturally superior to hers, and she was eager to listen to
him and learn.

Frederic would often find a reason for coming to the Conservatory and visiting Professor Soliva's singing class, where
Konstancya and her friend Mademoiselle Volkov were the

outstanding pupils. Frederic accompanied them on the piano,
and in the evenings entertained them with his improvisations.
But when he played the Adagio from the F minor *Concerto*
and the little *Waltz* (mentioned in his letter to Titus), he
meant them for Konstancya alone: through this music he
hoped to convey to her the feelings he did not yet dare to
express in words.

Frederic's happiness was soon marred, however, by jealousy.
Professor Soliva saw no reason why all admirers of his pupils,
even though not connected with the Conservatory, should be
prevented from paying calls. Frederic was annoyed by this
practice, and when he heard that two young Russian lieutenants from the Grand Duke's retinue were showing special
interest in Konstancya, he grew jealous and despondent. He
withdrew into himself. He remained in his room and tried to
find consolation in writing long letters to Titus.

"I would gladly dismiss the thoughts that poison my happiness, yet I delight in indulging them," he wrote him. "I
don't know myself what I want." He even applied for a passport and was ready to leave Warsaw.

Frederic was devoted to Titus, who, though his own age,
was a far more experienced person. Healthy and strong, he
had a realistic attitude toward problems both personal and
general. After his graduation from school, Titus had to
return to his estate, some two hundred miles from Warsaw,
to supervise the sowing and selling of the wheat as well as the
marketing of lambs and their wool, and of the products of his
distillery. But he was also an enthusiastic amateur musician,
and played the piano. Titus was a sympathetic friend, and
Frederic valued his advice and criticism above that of all
others. He longed to see him, to show him his compositions,
to discuss his plans, and perhaps even to confide the anguish
that tormented him.

Frederic hoped that Titus would come to Warsaw at the

end of May when Czar Nicholas I was expected to make a
visit. All sorts of celebrations and musical and theatrical performances were scheduled for the occasion. But Titus did not
come, and Frederic kept away from the festivities arranged
for the Czar's sojourn in Warsaw.

Frederic was a patriot, and he hated the Russians for robbing
Poland of its freedom. Now the two lieutenants were court-
ing Konstancya, and Frederic's resentment deepened into
hatred for everything Russian. He even went so far as to
stop seeing some of his old Russian friends. When the Russian authorities got word, Frederic was not invited to the
court concert at the Palace. "People must have been wonder-
ing why I was not there," he wrote Titus, "but I wasn't
surprised a bit."

While he did not attend a single performance honoring the
Czar, not even those in which Konstancya participated, he
could not let patriotism keep him from hearing Henrietta
Sontag, considered the greatest singer of her time.

The twenty-four-year-old soprano had a phenomenal, triumphal career. She was born in an actors' family, and, as often
happens in such cases, she was on the stage at the age of six.
Later, when her voice developed, she was applauded for its
beauty and her great musicianship. Frederic was dazzled by
her, but words failed him when he hurried to share his
impressions with Titus. "It seems that she breathes some
perfume of the freshest flowers into the audience," he wrote
rapturously. Yet he did add a single note of criticism: "She
caresses voluptuously but rarely moves one to tears."

Frederic was very proud to be introduced to Henrietta by
Prince Radziwill. Always susceptible to a woman's beauty, he
was even more drawn by her charm and kindness. He visited
her often, and one day was surprised to find Professor Soliva
there with Konstancya and Mademoiselle Volkov, getting
severe but constructive criticism from the great singer.

"She urged them to come to see her more often, so she could show them her own methods. This is more than natural kindness," Frederic remarked, overcome by a generosity not often found among popular artists. What Frederic did not know was that two years before this visit to Warsaw, Henrietta had secretly married Count Rossi, a diplomat, had given up her career for the sake of his, and now sang only on special occasions—thus she no longer had any reason to fear the competition of other young singers.

Frederic was very happy to be welcomed at the informal "lessons" Henrietta was giving the two girls. From her practical illustrations he gained knowledge of phrasing, as well as of the problems and possibilities of vocal performance. But what pleased him much more was that these lessons with Henrietta led to even longer discussions with Konstancya. Frederic suddenly became so interested in vocal music that when Konstancya half jokingly suggested he write an opera, he thought seriously about it for the first time. Had such a work been written it would certainly have featured a leading role for Konstancya.

The young girl might have been flattered by Frederic's no longer hidden affections and impressed with the growing popularity of his name. But Konstancya remained rather aloof. Perhaps, as some have suspected, she was warned not to take the whole thing seriously because of his poor health, and was reminded of his sister Emilia's death from the very disease that afflicted Frederic. Perhaps she was told that despite his early successes he might always remain poor like so many musicians, and would not be able to support her own career.

Konstancya said nothing when Frederic spoke of his plans to go abroad—not a single word about how much she would miss him, something Frederic had hoped to hear. When he asked her to give him something for a keepsake, she simply gave him a ribbon.

Somehow nothing seemed to disturb Frederic's feelings for her; he even cherished the ribbon. At times he was deliriously happy, and at others he would write to Titus: "When I think about it, I feel so sorry for myself that I become completely distracted. I might be run over by horses, and I would not know it."

But fortunately for him and everybody else Frederic kept working. He worked very hard, and to this period in his life, the last months of 1830, belong some of his important compositions. He wrote several *Mazurkas*, the *Ecossaises*, the *Polonaise in F minor* (Opus 71, Number 3), the *Introduction and Polonaise for cello and piano*, and—perhaps the most important—his *Piano Concerto in E minor*. Although this concerto was written after the one in F minor, it was the first published, and is therefore always called his first piano concerto.

At this time he also started the *Andante spianato,* to which he later added a *Polonaise,* but he did not finish it because he decided to go to Vienna and was too preoccupied with the preparations for his departure. Titus promised to join him on this journey, but Frederic could not decide on a date. There were several reasons for this. Europe was in political turmoil. Open revolts were reported in France, Italy, even Austria. And the never-dormant Polish patriots made everyone aware of their activities, which obviously were to lead sooner or later to armed revolt against the Russians. Merely to obtain a passport for travel abroad became a problem, and several times Frederic had to postpone his departure.

For sentimental reasons as well as to earn traveling money, Frederic decided to give a "Farewell Concert," in which he asked Konstancya and her friend Mademoiselle Volkov to take part.

The preparations took time. And Frederic was in a sad mental state: he hated to part with his family to whom

WARSAW.
On the left is the
Warsaw School
of Music.

he was devoted, and to break away from his circle of friends. He wrote to Titus that he had a strange premonition: "It seems to me that I am leaving home never to return, that I am going away to die. How sad it must be to die far from the place where one has spent his life. . . ."

Finally, on October 11, 1830, he gave his concert, his last in Poland. He had arranged the program so that he shared the next to last part with Konstancya. She looked lovely in her long white dress, he said, and she wore roses entwined in her

blond hair. Frederic believed that the audience was breathlessly listening to her rendition of O *quante lagrime per te versai* ("Oh, how many tears have I wept for you"), the cavatina from Rossini's *La Donna del lago*, because they were realizing the special meaning of it for these two young people.

Frederic planned to leave a few days after the concert, but he lingered on for several weeks. He paid one more visit to the Skarbeks at Zelazowa Wola, and spent many long evenings with his friends in Warsaw.

But what about Konstancya? He arranged with Jan Matuszynski, his former classmate, to pass on his letters to her.
Frederic's last rendezvous with her took place in a deserted
walk in the Saxon Park.

No one knows what the two said to each other during those
last few moments together—the young Kolberg, another friend
of Frederic's, was at the entrance protecting them from intru-
sion. Their parting can only be judged from Frederic's final
gesture: he gave her an old-fashioned wedding ring, a diamond
set in a silver band.

On the following day a stagecoach driven by four horses and
large enough for twelve passengers, carried only one. On the
outskirts of Warsaw it was stopped by a group of young people
singing:

> Nurtured on the soil of Poland
> May your fame ring through the world!

These were Frederic's friends from the Conservatory, led
by Professor Elsner. A few more parting words, and Elsner
bade him Godspeed, pressing into his hand a small package.
It contained some Polish soil, with which he was never to
part. When, nineteen years later, Frederic was buried in Paris,
this handful of soil was sprinkled over his coffin.

TITUS joined Frederic in Kalisz, Poland, and the two friends continued their journey to Vienna by the road already known to Frederic. It took them over two weeks to reach the Austrian capital, for in those days of traveling by stagecoach people took their time, stopped for several days in the cities of interest, visited museums and art galleries, and went to concerts and the opera. Also, it was not unusual for people to pay their respects at the estates of some aristocrats en route, even if these visits delayed their arrival at the principal destination for days.

In Wroclaw, which he knew well, Titus took Frederic to the opera, and in Dresden, where he had been on his last trip from Vienna, Frederic was eager to share his enthusiasm for his favorite paintings in the famous gallery. "When I see these pictures," he said to Titus, "it is as though I were hearing music."

They visited several Polish noblemen, and at the home of Countess Komar met three of her daughters. The twenty-three-year-old Delphine, the most beautiful one, had recently left her husband, Count Mieczyslav Potočki, and was planning to go to Paris, which she considered more of a music center than Vienna. She was an amateur musician herself. At that time, though, when Frederic's thoughts were preoccupied with Konstancya, Delphine made no particular impression on him.

Upon their arrival in Vienna, Frederic and Titus moved into a rather luxurious apartment on Kohlmarkt, which they had rented from Countess Lachmanowicz, an acquaintance in Warsaw.

Remembering the success of Frederic's previous visit to Vienna, one of the piano manufacturers had placed a piano at his disposal. With Titus to take charge of procuring the tickets for operas and concerts, and to schedule their social engagements, Frederic had every reason to look forward to a productive and successful start in the city. Even the cold which he had caught during their journey did not dampen his spirits. He was daydreaming about Konstancya, and in his letter to Matuszynski asked him of her: "Am I loved?"

Barely a week passed, when Titus and he heard disturbing news from Warsaw. A revolt had broken out against Russia, and Polish patriots were calling all Poles to arms. Suddenly, the pictures of earlier insurrections in which his father had taken part were awakened in Frederic's memory. He recalled stories of the ruthless way the Russians had crushed the up-risings, and of how later these foreign tyrants had used spies and persecution to try to rob the Poles of their national pride and their right to freedom.

Frederic wrote home that he would return at once, but his family advised him to remain in Vienna.

Titus and he followed and discussed every bit of news that reached them. When it became obvious that the struggle for independence would take time, that the rebels needed men in their ranks, Titus decided to join the patriots. But he, too, opposed Frederic's return to Poland. Frederic was much too frail and sickly to be a soldier. Like his parents and his friends,

Titus tried to persuade Frederic that he could best serve the cause of his nation by doing exactly what he was born to do: to speak of his people through his music.

But Frederic still yearned to join his friends active in the revolt. After Titus had departed, he felt so dejected, so alone, so completely lost, that he packed some of his belongings and took another stagecoach, hoping to overtake him. He failed in his pursuit, though, and finally returned to Vienna.

Left by himself, he no longer could afford the luxurious apartment. He moved to a more modest one on the top floor of the house. His hopes of earning some money by giving a concert or two vanished: Count Gallenberg, his enthusiastic admirer, was no longer the director of the Kärtnertor theater, and the man who took his place was not willing to pay Frederic, since he had played twice before without any charge.

Haslinger, the publisher, kept promising, but so far had always postponed publishing and paying for Frederic's works. Frederic was in such a nervous, depressed state that he could not compose or practice the piano. He craved company, friends. But Würfel was seriously ill with a pulmonary ailment, the Blahetkas had gone to Stuttgart, some of his friends among the Polish exiles had gone to France, and others had gone to join the patriots in Poland. Occasionally Frederic attended concerts, but these he found mediocre. Nothing could distract him from his thoughts of Poland, of his family and his friends who were fighting for their liberty there.

For no other apparent reason than that her first name was Konstancya, Frederic was drawn in Vienna to the home of a certain Madame Bayer.

All her music, handkerchiefs and linens are marked with *her* name [he wrote to Matuszynski, who was to relate everything to Konstancya]. My God, she and my sisters can make themselves useful at least by making bandages, and I? . . . Tell her that as long as my strength endures, until death, and even after my death,

my ashes will lie under her feet. But everything you could say
would still not be enough. . . . I'll write her myself! I would have
written long ago, I would not have tormented myself so long, but
for what people might say. If by any chance my letter should fall
into the hands of a stranger, it might harm her reputation, so it's
better that you speak for me.

Abduction of Polish
children by the Russians
(*Lithograph by
Engelmann*)

The following four months in Vienna were the most difficult
in Frederic's life. It never was in his nature to make his own
decisions. He was torn between what he wanted to do and
what he could do.

The situation in Poland changed constantly. After the
initial success of the patriots' armies, they suffered decisive

defeats, and the jubilant atmosphere gave way to general gloom and pessimism. Even the correspondence with his family and friends became more and more difficult. Titus was at the front, and so were all his other former classmates. Finally he heard that, seeking safety, his family had moved to Zelazowa Wola, and Konstancya with her family had left Warsaw. Matuszynski joined the army, and with him went Frederic's only tie with Konstancya.

He tormented himself by imagining Poland devastated, cities and villages burned and pillaged, his family and his friends murdered; he wished he were dead. The Austrians had no sympathy for the Polish cause, so the time was not favorable for his appearance as a Polish composer or even as a pianist. He knew he should go elsewhere. But where? Italy was in a state of unrest. France was the only country where Poles were treated with sympathy. Frederic decided to go to Paris.

First, he had to obtain a passport for travel to France, and to get this he needed permission from the Russian Embassy; Frederic, to all intents and purposes, was a Russian subject. It is easy to imagine his disgust when he saw that on his passport he was referred to as a *Russian* pianist.

On the way to Paris, Frederic stopped in Stuttgart.

He had been there only a few days when he learned that the Polish resistance had been crushed and the Russians once again occupied Warsaw. Frederic was heartsick. To calm his nerves during those long evenings and nights alone in a strange city, he worked on the unfinished *Scherzo in B minor* (Opus 20), and must have started his *Ballade in G minor* (Opus 23). Then, laying everything aside, he composed an *Etude in C minor* (Opus 10)—the famous *Revolutionary Etude*. It was his way of saying "Poland has not perished yet."

Frederic had made up his mind: he would go to Paris and try to make his life there. He would return to Poland when Poland was free.

PART TWO
1831~1849

8

*I*N less than two weeks after his arrival Frederic felt completely at home in Paris—and this despite the city's foreign atmosphere, so unlike that of any place he had ever known. Paris in the last century, just as today, startled newcomers from the German-speaking countries with its exuberance. The Parisians seemed always to be celebrating their freedom, as if they had just won it at last on the previous day.

To a sensitive musician accustomed to hearing voices subdued or even hushed from fear of being overheard and spied upon, the gaiety of Paris must have been a revelation.

The noise from the avenues crowded with open-air shops and sidewalk cafés and restaurants assailed and excited Frederic. Somehow, in Paris he instinctively realized what it meant to be a free man. It meant a great deal to Frederic, who was still brooding over Poland's loss of liberty.

He hastened to share his first impressions with Titus:

It is the greatest splendor, the greatest vileness, the greatest virtue and greatest vice. Here is more noise, clamor, clatter, and dirt than can be imagined. One gets lost in this paradise, but lost comfortably, because no one cares how anyone else lives. One can walk in rags in the street and yet at the same time frequent the best company. One day you eat an abundant dinner for thirty-two *sous* in a restaurant with mirrors, gold, and bright gas illumination, and the next day you may lunch at a place where they serve you portions fit for a bird and charge three times as much. . . . Paris is everything your heart desires—you may divert yourself, laugh, weep, do anything you please, and no one will pay any attention, for there are thousands doing the same thing as you, and each in his own way.

Paris at the time was the center of European culture. Victor Hugo, Heinrich Heine, Alfred de Vigny, Meyerbeer, Delacroix, Cherubini, Liszt, Rossini, and Balzac, to name only a few, all made their homes there. Frederic must have felt like a country boy visiting a capital for the first time, like a peasant bewildered by his first glimpse of city lights. Eager to be part of this alluring environment, he took the initative, though cautiously. He had to: he had very little money left and, as an unknown musician, needed access to Paris society. Who but the wealthy art patrons could sponsor his concerts or find him a few pupils?

It is true that in less than a week he met several famous musicians, among them the pianist Friedrich Kalkbrenner, who was then at the height of his fame. Frederic was very much impressed with Kalkbrenner's technique: faultless, effortless, and elegant, with what Frederic described as a "magical touch." In turn, Kalkbrenner, while he thought Frederic still had a great deal to learn, admired his playing and offered to give him lessons free of charge.

He had proposed that I should study with him for three years [Frederic wrote to his parents, asking their advice in this matter], then he would make something out of me, something quite special. . . . He told me that I lack schooling, that I am on the road to becoming an excellent pianist, but that I might go astray, that there will be no representative of a great piano school after

A street in Paris in the 1830 s

he dies or stops playing, but that I could not found a new school, even if I wanted to, without knowing the old. He also said that my compositions have character, that it would be a pity if I did not fulfill my promise, etc. etc.

Always reluctant to make a decision, Frederic waited for a reply from his parents, Titus, and Elsner. They were unanimously against the proposition. They suspected that Kalkbrenner's offer was purely selfish; he wanted to boast that Chopin was his product, they said. Meanwhile Frederic was continually meeting other musicians, and he sought their

advice before making a final decision. Liszt was against it, and Mendelssohn said simply: "You won't learn anything from him. You play better than he does."

Yet Frederic, who recognized his own shortcomings, decided to study with Kalkbrenner. To pacify his family and friends in Poland he wrote, referring to his lessons: "I still ride in my own coach—I have only hired a coachman for the horses."

Kalkbrenner had indeed underestimated Frederic's talent. Before long their lessons became mere discussions between two artists, Kalkbrenner perhaps learning from them as much as Frederic. Through Kalkbrenner, Frederic widened the circle of his acquaintances and friends, but he missed Titus.

I wish that you were here [he wrote him, although he knew that his friend could not leave Poland]. You won't believe how sad I am because I have no one to confide in. You know how easily I make friends, how I like to talk with them about nothing at all— and I have such friends, more than I can count, but no one with whom I can share my feelings. That's why I get tired, and you won't believe how much I crave some respite, a whole day when no one will be talking to me.

He confessed to Titus that his health was poor, that his gaiety when he was among "his own kind" (he meant the Poles, of whom there was a large colony in Paris), was merely a façade. He said something was constantly gnawing at him: premonitions, anxieties, dreams or insomnia, nostalgia or utter indifference.

Frederic was so downhearted that at times he seemed to be losing the will to live. A mixture of emotions made him bitter, and tormented him with memories that only aggravated his state of mind. And no wonder: he saw his money—what little there was left—dwindling away, and there was no chance of earning any more, since he had none to go into that world of high society where lay his only chance of finding someone to sponsor a concert.

And the news of Konstancya only deepened his dejection. His younger sister Isabella wrote him that Konstancya had married Joseph Grabowski, a wealthy Polish landowner, adding that she herself had found Konstancya to be an egotistical, calculating young woman. Her letter aroused all sorts of doubts about Konstancya in Frederic's mind. He remembered that she had met Grabowski while he was still in Warsaw. Had she then been only pretending to love Frederic? Was it all false? And if she did have any true feelings, did she save them only for her music?

His dream of happiness, which he had nurtured in his heart for several years, was shattered; Frederic never mentioned

Konstancya again. He never knew that she became the mother of five children, and at the age of thirty-five went completely blind. Shortly before she died, at nearly eighty years old, she destroyed all Frederic's letters and souvenirs, including an ivory miniature of him with which she had never parted.

The end of his relationship with Konstancya in 1831 completed the first half of his life. Frederic realized that if he were to live, even as he had been during these first five months in Paris, he had to make a new start regardless of the odds against him. He knew he could not compete on the concert stage with the virtuosos who had already conquered the Parisian audiences. He had no means for publicity: his name, Frederic Chopin, a pianist from Warsaw, meant nothing and would not draw a large public. But he had to give a concert for better or worse. He went to as many well-known artists as he could and asked them to participate with him in the performance. Kalkbrenner led the list.

Finally, after several postponements, Frederic, white as a sheet and nervously rubbing his cold hands, made his debut on February 26, 1832, in a hall only half-filled—mostly by his friends and the Polish refugees who came out of patriotic feeling.

The net result of this concert was not very encouraging. Since Kalkbrenner had arranged to have the hall free of charge, and Frederic did not have to pay those who participated on the program, he made a little money. But François-Joseph Fétis, the Belgian musicologist, and the most eminent music critic in Paris, though he praised the originality of Frederic's compositions, pointed out "a lack of order in the sequence of phrases, so that at times one seems to be hearing improvisation rather than written music."

This he attributed to Frederic's youth, and said he believed that with experience he would win "a brilliant and well merited reputation."

FREDERIC CHOPIN
(*Portrait by Ary Scheffer*)

Speaking of Frederic as a pianist, he gave him credit for elegant playing which had brilliance and clarity, but suggested that "the study he is making under Kalkbrenner cannot fail to give him an important quality on which finesse of execution depends." Thus Fétis repeated what Kalkbrenner had said. The tone of his critical column did nothing to lift Frederic's spirit. It spoke of a fulfilled promise, if and when, but offered no foundation for a successful present.

Frederic's second public appearance at a charity concert two months later did not win a better reaction from the press. This time Fétis, again reviewing his performance of the F minor *Concerto*, pointed to "the small amount of sound M. Chopin draws from the piano"—the kind of criticism which was always to plague Frederic.

During the following summer months Paris was threatened by an epidemic of cholera. Most of Frederic's friends fled from the city, leaving him lonely and discouraged.

Frederic realized that his initial appearance had failed to win

the Paris audience, and he now decided to try his luck somewhere else—perhaps in London or in the United States. From
his friends in the Polish refugee circle he heard a great deal
about the land that offered unlimited opportunities, and he
often listened to those who planned to emigrate to America.
He even wrote about it to his family. But they were aghast at
the idea of his going so far. Instead, his father suggested that
he return to Warsaw. But Frederic would not hear of it, not
until the rule in Poland had been overthrown.

Then, as if guided by Providence, Frederic ran into Prince
Valentin Radziwill one day on the street. The Prince was a
relative of Antoni, his admirer and friend in Warsaw. Frederic
confided the true state of his affairs and said he had decided to
go to America. The Prince was just as aghast as his family. He
advised Frederic not to be hasty, and within a few days took
him to a brilliant soiree at the home of Baron James de
Rothschild.

This was the turning point in Frederic's life and career. For
Baron de Rothschild was not only a member of the well-known
dynasty of bankers, but he and his family were great patrons
of the arts. Frederic's playing enchanted an audience of aristocrats and select members of Paris high society. Baroness de
Rothschild played the piano herself, and was the first to ask
Frederic to give her lessons. Many others followed. Suddenly
Frederic was being entertained in diplomatic and financial
circles. In a letter to Dominik Dzievanovski, his former classmate at whose family estate at Szafarino he had spent two
happy summers, he described the sudden change in his fortune:

I have entered the highest society. I sit among ambassadors,
princes, and ministers, and I don't know by what miracle this came
to pass, because I myself made no effort to get there. It is very
important for me . . . the moment you have been heard at the
English or Austrian embassy, they assume you have a great talent
. . . that you play better if Princess Vaudemont (the last of the

old Montmorency family) is your protector. . . . If I were more
stupid than I am, I would think that I am at the peak of my
career, but I realize how much remains to be done, and I realize
it all the more because I am close to the foremost artists and I
know what each of them is lacking. . . . If you haven't forgotten
what I'm like, you will know that I am the same today as I was
yesterday, with this difference—that I have one side whisker, while
the other refuses to grow. I have to give five lessons today. You'd
think I am making a fortune. But a carriage and white gloves,
without which a man has no *bon ton*, cost more than I have. At
heart I am a revolutionary—hence I care not at all for money, but
only for friendship.

It was not long before Frederic found a publisher, Maurice
Schlesinger, who brought out his latest works, written since
he had come to France: four *Mazurkas* (Opus 6) and five
Mazurkas (Opus 7). Now, with an assured income from publication and his teaching, Frederic could afford to leave his very
modest lodgings on the Boulevard Poissonnière and take an
apartment at 4, Cité Bergère.

9

*F*REDERIC'S fortunes certainly improved. After giving his daily quota of lessons, he would change into immaculately tailored clothes and ride in his carriage to dine and spend the evening at the home of a prince or princess, an ambassador, or a wealthy banker. But of all his hosts and hostesses he preferred Countess Delphine Potocka.

He had already met her once at the home of her parents in Dresden, when Titus and he visited the city on their way to Vienna. Although he had known all along that the Countess was in Paris, he was, because of his financial situation, too shy to call on her. Now it was different; on several occasions he met her at receptions and dinners at which he was an honored guest.

Frederic soon became her frequent visitor—and her piano teacher. The Countess, a great beauty to whom poets and painters often dedicated their works, was an unusually talented musician. With her beautiful soprano voice she could have made a career as a concert or opera singer, but she had no such ambitions. She played well enough to accompany herself, but she preferred to stand by the piano where her graceful figure could be in full view. She was always exquisitely dressed, with only one string of pearls as adornment.

The Countess showed such interest in her lessons that Frederic worked with her as he would have with an aspiring professional.

It has always been of much interest to pianists and piano teachers to study the way in which masters such as Liszt and Chopin taught their pupils. Thereby one not only learns their method of practice, but one also comes to a closer understanding of their compositions. Liszt lived much longer than Chopin, so some of our contemporary pianists have been fortunate enough to study under Liszt's pupils. But among the few pupils of Chopin's students none has survived. Therefore a few words of his advice to Potočka are of value.

Once again I repeat [he wrote to Potočka, who was away from Paris], don't play more than two hours a day—that is quite enough during the summer. I won't send you my "Etudes"; you must play them for the first time with me, and after hearing how Liszt plays them. That will be best, because if you interpret them incorrectly, you'll have to unlearn them; but after listening to Liszt you'll have the ideal picture. And I fear that by playing the "Etudes" before I show you how to practice them you will tire your hands for good, which might easily happen. You see, my "Etudes" are a new method in exercise, and it can be treacherous and dangerous for the uninitiated.

Then, giving her more general advice, he said:

Be careful with the pedal, because this is a sensitive and noisy rascal. You must treat it delicately and with respect—as a friend it is most helpful, but not easily does one win its friendship and love.

He spoke against the established rules of fingering:

To an accomplished virtuoso all tricks are permitted. He should use his own methods by all means. You may put your thumb under your little finger, if it is an advantage in the execution of the passages. If necessary, take two white or even two black keys with one finger. If you put the third finger over the fourth or even the fifth, you won't be committing a mortal sin either. Don't tire the fourth finger too much; it is so closely connected with the third that you'll never succeed in making it quite independent. My fourth finger is completely untrained, yet I can manage it in such a way that no one would notice. Each finger is built differently; each has a different strength and function. One mustn't destroy but on the contrary develop the subtlety of touch that is proper and natural to each finger.

Play Bach's "Preludes" and "Fugues" every day. This is the best school; no one will ever create a better. If you have plenty of time, memorize Bach; only by memorizing a work does one become thoroughly acquainted with it. Without Bach you cannot have freedom in the fingers, nor a clear and beautiful tone. A pianist who doesn't recognize Bach is a fool.

Bach will never become old. His works are written like those

Delphine Potočka
as a girl

ideally conceived geometric figures in which everything is in its
proper place and not a single line is superfluous. . . . When I play
another composer's work, I often think that I would have solved
or written this or that passage in a different way. But when I play
Bach, I never feel like this. Everything he does is perfect; it is not
possible to imagine it otherwise, and the slightest change would
spoil everything.

Frederic also revealed to Countess Potočka that while he
was composing his *Etudes*, he had at the same time been
seriously contemplating some studies—he called them "exercises"—less difficult and for less advanced students of piano.

In writing my "Etudes" I tried to put to use not only science
but also art. Since a virtuoso must practice for a long time, he
should be given exercises in which he will find "proper food for his
ears and his soul, lest he be bored to death. I am disturbed because
there are no beautiful exercises for beginners. A virtuoso has everything open to him; when he is bored with exercises, he can reach
out for the most beautiful music. But a poor fellow who cannot
play anything except exercises, whose fingers are as though tied,
needs beautiful exercises that will save him from becoming dis-
gusted with music. I have tried to write something of this kind,
but I haven't been successful, because for the beginner everything
is difficult. Perhaps I'll postpone this work until later, or maybe
someone else will forestall me. It's quite difficult.

Frederic also told her—and this despite Kalkbrenner's opinion that he could not found his own method—that he was
planning to write just such a work for piano students, *A
Method of Methods*.

Do you know [he wrote to Potočka], that my letters to you are
the beginning of another, perhaps greater work? I want to write
about music and the art of the piano, because we lack such books,
but I don't know whether I am equal to such an undertaking,
because it is easier for me to write "notes" than "letters." In writing
to you I practice writing about music.

Unfortunately, Frederic never accomplished these two tasks. Nothing was found among his papers after his death, and these paragraphs in letters to Potočka are his only reference to the planned work. It is certainly a great loss. He need not have been inhibited by any lack of literary style, for he always expressed himself well and clearly, and in fact both Balzac and George Sand, the famous French novelists who knew him well, said he had a talent for writing.

According to some meager information left to us by his pupils, he demanded strict adherence to the prescribed tempi, but within this metronomic precision he insisted on that complete freedom of expression that has its musical term—*rubato*. Only in this way do Chopin's own compositions become alive.

Although he wrote no vocal music, he learned a great deal from Henrietta Sontag's lessons to Konstancya and from all

HENRIETTA SONTAG

the operas and vocal concerts he had attended. He knew that melody was born from the human voice, that it was governed by breathing, and that the knowledge of when to sustain the melody and when to take a fresh breath were the prerequisites of correct phrasing, and, hence, free execution—*rubato*. This unerring sense must have been to Chopin the foundation of musicianship.

Frederic's letters to Countess Potocka reveal that she was more to him than just another pupil. She was his closest friend, his confidante; above all, she was one of the few who could have been called an "inspiration." She was the only woman in his life to whom he paid this tribute: "My longing for you begot in me many musical ideas." Frederic dedicated several works to her, and always sought her reaction to pieces he was in the midst of composing. While she was at her summer home at Enghien, he wrote her: "I won't send my finished 'Etudes' to your lake. I would rather play them to you myself for the first time. I want to see whether any of them will turn out to be special favorites of us both, as the E major is." This is the work about which Liszt is supposed to have said that he would give all his own compositions for its first eight bars. "Do you remember the piece," Frederic asked Potocka, "which I improvised when we had quarreled and made up, three days before you left? It has become my *Etude in E-flat Major*. I am sure you'll like it."

Their quarrel could not have been serious, for no dramatic element is reflected in this piece. On the contrary, it is a very lyrical work, as if it had been written for the harp. But then no artistic inspiration needs to be mirrored programmatically in a composition (see Appendix).

❧ 10 ❧

*D*URING the next two years, Frederic's fame grew steadily. His life took on a regular pattern. He rose late, and was attended by a barber and valet. After midday he was ready to begin his teaching. In the evening he changed into a white shirt with flowing silk tie, a black frock coat, and gray trousers. White gloves in hand, he would descend to the carriage waiting at the door to take him for an evening's entertainment. His popularity in society was such that the Parisian salons vied with one another to have the honor and pleasure of his company. But now Frederic could afford to be particular about where he went. Also, he no longer felt he had to perform wherever he was invited "to pay for his dinner." There is a well-known story about one of his hosts who kept urging Frederic to play after dinner, until Frederic, annoyed, told him that he "had not enjoyed the dinner that much." Frederic could afford to say this, for he was one of the first musicians to be received in society as the equal of other guests. Until then, musicians had been treated little better than servants.

Frederic still participated occasionally in public concerts, but the more he played the less he liked it. "I am not fit for

FRANZ LISZT

concerts," he said to Liszt. "Crowds intimidate me. I feel poisoned by their breath, paralyzed by curious glances, and confused by the sight of strange faces."

During this busy time, the list of his compositions continued to grow, and now they were often played in public by others besides himself: Liszt, Kalkbrenner, and, in Germany, Clara Wieck, later to be Robert Schumann's wife. Frederic had every reason to be satisfied with the career he had made for himself in so short a time.

Every summer he was invited to spend his vacation with friends: in 1834 he received two such invitations—one to attend a music festival in Aachen, Germany, and the other to visit Count Wodzinski's family in Geneva. This second invitation brought back the past for Frederic: the three Wodzinski boys had been his classmates, and he had taught their sister the piano when they all still lived in Warsaw.

The Wodzinskis were rich, and, like so many other aristocrats, they left Warsaw during the uprising that took place shortly after Frederic arrived in Vienna. Now they divided their time between Dresden and Geneva. Frederic had heard news of them through mutual friends, but this invitation was the first direct word he had received. With her invitation, the Countess sent him a short composition by his former pupil, Maria.

I was extremely pleased with it [Frederic wrote to Felix, Maria's brother]. That very same evening I improvised on a pretty little theme of Maria's composition, that Maria whom I used to chase through your apartment in the good old days . . . shouting "I love you, I love you." And today! I take the liberty of sending my esteemed colleague Mademoiselle Maria a little Waltz that I have just published [Opus 18]. I hope it will give her at least one hundredth part of the pleasure I felt on receiving her "Variations."

When he wrote these words, Frederic could not have suspected that there would be a sequel to this invitation. He was unable to accept the Wodzinskis' because he had already agreed to go to Aachen.

The following summer he was vacationing at Enghien, Potočka's favorite resort, when he heard from his parents that they were on their way to Carlsbad where his father intended to undergo a cure. He had not seen his parents for five years, and so far as he knew, this chance of seeing them outside of Poland might be his only opportunity. The journey to Carlsbad would take only two nights and a day by stagecoach. Frederic left immediately.

It would not be difficult to imagine the joy this meeting brought the family.

My dear children [he wrote to his sisters]. This is the first letter you have ever received written by both Papa and myself. Our joy is indescribable! We hug and hug each other—and what else can one do? It's a pity we cannot all be together. What I write is chaotic; today it is better not to think, but only to enjoy our happiness. This is the only thing that exists for me today. Papa and Mama are exactly the same, only they've aged a little . . . we talk about you, we say how often we have thought of one another. We drink and eat together; we pamper and scold each other. The same habits, the same gestures I grew up with, the same hand that I have not kissed for so long. Well, my children, I embrace you— and forgive me for being unable to collect my thoughts and write you about anything except our happiness at this moment, except that I have always hoped for this happiness, and that today I really have it, this happiness, happiness.

The three weeks flew by like a day. When the time came for his parents to return to Warsaw, Frederic accompanied them as far as the Polish border. He was never to see them again.

With a heavy heart he started the journey back to Paris, which, by chance, took him through Dresden. There Frederic called on the Wodzinskis. He found the whole family at home; the three boys, Maria, her two younger sisters, and their parents. They were delighted to see him, proud of his success, and eager to hear all about his life in Paris, and to hear his compositions. Frederic shared everything with them joyously. He had just passed nearly a month in a warm family atmosphere, something he had missed for many years, and now the Countess took him in as if he were her own son. In fact she called him her "fourth" boy.

But it was with Maria that Frederic spent most of his time in Dresden. At eighteen she was perhaps not the prettiest girl he had ever seen, but her childlike charm made her very attractive. She was well educated, and showed a definite talent for painting as well as music. She had a pleasant alto voice, played the piano well enough to participate in charity concerts, and even composed. There is no doubt that after his sophisticated friends in Paris Frederic found Maria's innocence especially appealing. And he must have thought about it very often when he returned to Paris a few days later.

MARIA WODZINSKA

He had been away a whole summer from his established musical life, his work, and his associations with colleagues —except for a one-day visit with Mendelssohn, Clara Wieck, and Schumann when he passed through Leipzig on the way home.

In Paris he found the musical season already in full swing. Sigismund Thalberg, a newcomer among the pianists, was challenging Liszt's supremacy. Frederic kept himself aloof from such competition. He devoted more and more thought to his compositions, though with half of his mind he dwelt on Maria. In a few letters she spoke of how much the whole family missed him, but he read "between the lines"; could Maria truly be fond of him? The thought, the hope filled his mind.

It is doubtful that he spoke about it to anyone, not even to Potocka. At the time, the Countess had decided suddenly to leave Paris and return to her husband. Frederic, in his fear of loneliness, needed someone to turn to for friendship; naturally Maria was his first choice.

For some time Frederic had been thinking of marriage, and children of his own. If it had been possible he would have married Potočka, but she was married already. He wanted to settle down in one place and devote himself to composing and teaching, with perhaps an occasional concert appearance when absolutely necessary.

Now that he had felt the warmth of his family again and heard about the marriages of his sisters and Titus, Frederic was touched by the poignance of his bachelor life.

But of course the wife he chose would have to be a Pole. Frederic could not think of speaking to his wife and children in any other language than Polish. On that subject he was very stern with Potočka, who considered French the only language to use in letters. He compromised by letting her "spice" them with an occasional phrase in French.

Maria's social position played no small part in his choice of matrimonial ties. Frederic was most comfortable among aristocrats or the rich, and the Wodzinskis were both. He loved the patriarchal tradition that ruled their interests and tastes; he admired their exclusiveness. On the whole, he could not imagine any greater happiness than becoming a member of the Wodzinski family.

Frederic wrote his parents of his marriage intentions and asked his mother to join him in Dresden. As might have been expected, his family was pleased with his desire to marry, and particularly with his choice, though his father was a little doubtful about the success of his plan.

But by bad luck, Frederic fell seriously ill. He developed a high fever and coughed up blood. In fact, there were rumors, which even reached Warsaw, that he had died. Not wanting to upset his family, he wrote them only when he recovered, two months later. Again he spoke of going to Dresden.

However that may be [his father answered him], it is a beautiful castle in Spain. But never mind, let us keep building it. I think that if it can be made to come true at all, you cannot do better than with your mother at your side. But all this requires health and money, and you must begin to think of one and the other. This is the only way for you to see Dresden again and that which may interest you there.

But once more Frederic had to change his plans. He heard from Maria's brother that in July while their father was taking his sons to Poland to see about the management of one of their estates, their mother with her daughters would be visiting Marienbad. Frederic had no time to raise enough money through concerts for his mother's trip, but as he did not want to be handicapped by lack of funds in Marienbad, he worked feverishly on several new compositions which he hoped to sell to publishers before leaving.

All went well, as if fate were leading him to his happiness. In Marienbad he and the Wodzinskis lived in the same hotel. Frederic was closer to the family than ever before. At the end of August he accompanied them back to Dresden, and it was there that he planned to propose to Maria.

But he was timid, and did not express his intentions until the day before he had to leave Dresden to return to Paris. Maria gave him her consent, but asked him to speak about it to her mother.

Shortly before dinner, at twilight, which the Poles call the "gray hour," he summoned his courage and went to see the Countess. She happened to be suffering from a toothache, but during their short visit she indicated that she was not against the idea of a marriage. She asked Frederic to keep it secret, however, until she had gained the Count's consent.

What Frederic apparently did not realize was that the very qualities that attracted him to the Wodzinskis—their social position, title, exclusiveness—made his suit impossible. How could Maria marry the son of a schoolteacher, a poor musician by their standards, no matter how esteemed his name may have become in the artistic world? He did not know that the girl's uncle, an old and proud aristocrat, was already annoyed by Frederic's prolonged visits and constant attentions to Maria. And his brother, Maria's father, would not think of going against the old man's wishes.

Back in Paris, and unaware of all this, Frederic continued to correspond with the Wodzinskis—with the Countess particularly, who was concerned about his health; she was well informed about it and gave him motherly advice. As far as he could see there was no reason to worry. He was planning to join the family during the following summer, when his engagement—so far kept secret—would be made official.

Maria wrote that she was looking forward to the meeting with his family in Warsaw where the Wodzinskis were going in the spring of 1837. And the Wodzinskis did see the Chopins several times. Maria gave Ludwika a portrait of Frederic she had drawn while he was in Dresden. But during their visits neither family mentioned what was said at that "gray hour" by Frederic and the Countess.

The date of his meeting with Maria was again postponed from one season to another. The Countess' letters gradually became less personal and more general. Maria no longer wrote him except to add postscripts to her mother's letters, still expressing hope for happier days to come.

Then their correspondence became less frequent, and ceased altogether. Frederic's hopes, his "castle in Spain," had come crashing down. After his death a package containing all the Wodzinskis' letters was found. A faded rose, which Maria had given him when he parted with her in Dresden, was attached to it with a pink ribbon. Next to it were these words written by Frederic: *Moya beda*, which in Polish means roughly "my sorrow."

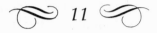

ONCE again Frederic moved to a new apartment, this time at 38, rue de la Chaussée d'Antin. Always concerned about living and working in the right atmosphere, he paid particular attention to its furnishing. He had developed extremely good taste—indeed, after so many visits to the beautiful homes of wealthy and aristocratic friends, it would be surprising if he had not. Merely having good taste, of course, would not have done much for him, but now he had the means to indulge in almost any luxury he felt his new home required.

He deliberated a long time until he found wallpaper the exact color he wanted both for his drawing room and bedroom: it was *tourterelle* (dove-colored), but bright and glossy, and bordered with dark green. In his sitting room, two carefully chosen red sofas and chairs were placed at the right distance from the grand piano and the fireplace to offer his guests both warmth and comfortable conditions for listening to music. The heavy gray curtains at the windows not only prevented the sharp light from intruding into the serene atmosphere of the drawing room, but, like the thick rugs on the floor, they mellowed the sound of the piano. Frederic loved violets, and his adoring pupils saw to it that his vases were always filled with fresh ones. And, as befitted a man so well situated, Frederic engaged a manservant who acted as a valet, cook, and sort of glorified secretary, one of whose duties was to keep out unannounced visitors when his master wanted to be alone.

While he still continued to attend receptions and dinner parties, Frederic now preferred to entertain at his own home. The evenings at the rue de la Chaussée d'Antin soon became well known in Paris, and it was an honor to belong to the circle of Frederic's intimate friends. Among these some have been forgotten, but others belong to the history of art, music, and literature: Eugène Delacroix, the French painter, Heinrich Heine, the German poet, Adam Mickiewicz, the Polish poet, and Julian Niemcewicz, the Polish novelist, mingled in Frederic's drawing room with Polish aristocrats and French bankers such as the de Rothschilds.

At one such evening, the guest list included George Sand, then an already well-known French novelist. George Sand was not a man, but a woman whose real name was Aurore Dupin. She took her masculine pen name because, at that time, readers of her novels would never have accepted the idea that their author was a woman. She had been married to Baron Dudevant, but she did not use her title. Her adopted name suited her personality and way of living much better. Like a man she wore trousers and jackets, and smoked cigars.

George Sand, as a woman of distinguished talent, was more welcome at the gatherings of the literati, artists, and musicians, where her eccentricities were accepted as a part of her personality, than at the homes of high Paris society.

Frederic had met Sand in Liszt's home. He probably would not have paid her much attention (she spoke few words during the evening) were it not for her dark eyes, smoothly combed black hair, and olive complexion. They reminded him of Maria. But his first impression was not favorable. "What an

"Giorgia S . . ." (*Drawing of George Sand by Alfred de Musset*)

unattractive, unpleasant person is this George Sand," he said
to a friend, as they were walking home after the party. "Is it
really a woman? I am inclined to doubt it."

As if to dispel his doubts, the first time Liszt brought her
to Frederic's apartment, she wore a white dress with a red
sash, the colors of the Polish flag. But again Sand sat by herself at the fireside, smoking cigars and not joining the guests'
conversation. Frederic was almost frightened of her.

Besides, he had not sufficiently recovered from the collapse
of his marriage plans to think of becoming involved with
another woman. It took Frederic some time to accept what
seemed to him utterly inconceivable—that the Wodzinskis'
final decision not to let their daughter become his wife was
based on the fact that he was neither a nobleman nor rich.
This hurt his pride, for he sincerely believed that his art and
what he stood for in Poland—the Wodzinskis' homeland as

well as his—should have been considered above all class prejudices. Perhaps it did not occur to him that his ill-health influenced their decision. Or was it possible that Maria was so completely controlled by her family and their traditions that she had no will of her own? Frederic finally had to accept the fact that this must have been so.

Again he had to seek solace in his work and in the general hubbub of the musical season in Paris, even if he were more an observer than an active participant. At that time Frederic saw Liszt more often than before, for Liszt, a past master in the art of publicity, never missed an opportunity to be present at social gatherings, to which Frederic was inevitably invited.

It has been assumed that Chopin and Liszt were great friends. Actually, as often happens with artists, they were jealous of each other, and this, of course, affected the sincerity of their relationship. Liszt's ability as a composer did not develop until much later, and at this time he was regarded merely as a great virtuoso; he envied Chopin the composer. As for Chopin, he envied Liszt's virtuosity, and often said: "I wish I could steal from him the way he plays my 'Etudes.'" After his first public performance he heard from Ernest Legouvé, a music critic, that Liszt would be reviewing the concert. "Please believe me, he would create a Kingdom for you," Legouvé said. "Yes, a Kingdom, but within his own Empire," Frederic answered.

When Sigismund Thalberg, the pianist, created a sensation in Paris, Frederic nonetheless sided with those who favored Liszt. "Thalberg plays beautifully. But he is not my man. He plays both soft and loud with the pedal but not with his hands. He spans ten notes as easily as I do eight. And he wears diamond studs in his shirt." It must have been gratifying for Frederic to hear that during that Thalberg-Liszt rivalry Heinrich Heine said: "I don't care . . . I think that Chopin plays better than either one."

In the fall of that year, 1837, Frederic, still depressed about Maria, often visited Liszt at his home, where he met George Sand again and again.

But George Sand did not remain in Paris all the time. She spent many months at her château at Nohant, a small village in central France, where she wrote prolifically. During her turbulent life she produced over one hundred volumes, the result of the most disciplined labor—even if at rather odd hours (she worked from midnight until five in the morning). Sand's home at Nohant, with its beautiful garden, offered her the ideal peace for writing; in fact, she planned to make it a home for other artists also, who could profit from the serenity of the place. Liszt was a frequent guest, and when he told her that he intended to bring Chopin to Nohant, she bought a beautiful Pleyel grand piano for him to use. But Chopin did not come. Later, George Sand made several trips to Paris, and, when she spent the whole of the following summer in the city, her casual acquaintance with Frederic grew into a close friendship.

Chopin and Sand were two distinct artistic personalities. Only through her patience and understanding of human relations could Sand overcome the differences in their characters, beliefs, tastes, and even their attitudes toward the arts and their work.

To begin with, George Sand was a foreigner to Chopin, whose Polish national feelings and traits were the basis of his nature. The French language, which he knew well, still was a foreign tongue to him, as he had already told Potocka. He spoke it with an accent and wrote it incorrectly. It is doubtful that he even read Sand's works; though she was as absorbed in her own writing as he was in his music, she could be, and was, a sympathetic listener.

Even their methods of working were different. Frederic was capable of rewriting, improving, and polishing some of his compositions for months and months, while George Sand would send her manuscripts to the publisher as soon as the last page was completed.

Socially, Chopin and Sand moved in different spheres: he among the aristocrats whose homes, tastes, and manners he admired and adopted; she among artists who cared nothing for luxury or position. Chopin's friends contributed, by their own example, to the reserve of his nature, his secretiveness, and his habit of careful deliberation over opinions. In contrast, George Sand was impulsive and proud of her straightforwardness, traits which were not simply tolerated but welcomed in the circle of her friends, where even common taste or vulgarity were not considered mortal sins. She epitomized eccentricity, and would accept any conditions life offered her; she was not afraid of them, while Chopin shrank from ugliness or pain. It was not easy for them to adjust these differences for the sake of their relationship, but it proved nonetheless to be one of the longest in Chopin's life.

At the time of his blossoming friendship with George Sand, Frederic was not at all well. The symptoms of his illness recurred often and kept him in bed more than before. His doctor assured him that he did not have tuberculosis, only an acute inflammation of the larynx. However, the same doctor said privately to George Sand: "If you could take him South you would prolong his life."

What Frederic needed was a long rest and affectionate care. And George Sand could provide him with both. At that time she was also worried about her son Maurice, who was suffering from rheumatism. She had been thinking of taking him to Italy for the winter. But after consulting with friends she chose Majorca, and invited Frederic to go along. To say that he agreed to do so only because he needed a warm climate and good care would be to underestimate George Sand's charm and his growing attachment for her.

I am in Palma, [Majorca] among palms, cedars, cacti, olives, oranges, lemons, figs, pomegranates, etc.—everything that the Jardin des Plantes [in Paris] has in its hothouses. The sky is like turquoise, the sea like lapis lazuli, the mountains emerald, the air is heavenly [Frederic wrote in the middle of November, 1838, to Julian Fontana, the Polish pianist, his old friend]. Sun all day, everyone wears summer clothes, it is hot; at night, guitars and singing for hours on end. Enormous balconies with grapevines overhead. Moorish walls. Everything turns its face toward Africa, as the whole town does. In a word, a marvelous life.

Frederic's happiness was not even marred by the discomforts of rustic life on the island. This was not Paris, or Vienna, or anything he had seen in Poland or Germany. It was an entirely different country, whose inhabitants had their own character and customs. There were no hotels in Palma, but George Sand managed to find and rent a villa.

All that was left of this "villa" was its pretty name, "Son Vent." There were neither doors nor windows; plaster was falling off the bare walls, and the furnishings consisted of a few old tables, straw chairs, and broken-down cots instead of beds. George Sand was not in the least disconcerted, and while trying to make their quarters livable organized walking excursions and picnics into the surrounding mountains to keep everybody in good spirits.

But, unfortunately, during one of these excursions, when they were still three miles away from home, a violent storm broke. Frederic returned soaking wet, and two days later developed such a bad cold that George Sand, frightened, called in the three best-known doctors in town.

They diagnosed his condition as acute bronchitis, and prescribed bloodletting. Both Frederic and Sand were against it, and dismissed the three of them.

After he had fully recovered Frederic described the doctors' visit to Fontana:

For the past two weeks I have been as sick as a dog: I got a chill, despite the temperature of 70, amidst roses, oranges, palms and fig trees. Of the three most famous doctors on the island, one sniffed at what I spat up, the other tapped at the place I spat from, and the third poked and listened while I spat it. The first said that I had already croaked, the second—that I was dying, and the third—that I shall die. And today I'm the same as always.

Frederic seemed to be far more worried over the lost time that delayed the *Preludes* he had promised his publisher in Paris. Also, the upright piano Camille Pleyel, the manufacturer, had offered to send him had not yet arrived. He would have so much enjoyed playing during those beautiful evenings of their first month on the island. But now the weather had changed to interminable rain and wind that blew with ghostly howls through the empty corridors and rooms.

News of Frederic's illness spread quickly among the islanders, making further stay in the villa impossible. As it was, the Majorcans were hostile to strangers. They refused to work for them, overcharged them in their stores, and in general made their lives as unpleasant as they could. But when they heard that Frederic was suffering from tuberculosis, a disease they feared as much as cholera, they were ready to chase them out of town. Their landlord demanded that they leave the villa immediately, claiming moreover that the place should be "disinfected" by a thorough cleaning and re-whitewashed at their expense. They had no other place to go except (as Frederic called it) "a huge old ruined Carthusian monastery" nearby.

During one of their excursions they had been so enchanted by the sight of this monastery perched on the side of a mountain, that Sand had immediately rented three cells which she thought could serve her and Frederic as an ideal place for working. Now they had no other refuge but this one, in Valdemosa, three miles away from Palma.

Since the monks had left two years before, only three persons

The monastery at Valdemosa *(Drawing by Sand's son, Maurice)*

still lived in the monastery: the gatekeeper, the former pharmacist who for some unknown reason had stayed on, and Maria Antonia, the cook, who now served meals to curious tourists. The monastery consisted of several buildings separated by small courtyards and gardens, a church and twelve chapels— now all deserted. The apartment that Sand had rented, consisting of three cells, was one of twelve identical apartments separated by low-vaulted and narrow corridors.

My cell has the shape of a tall coffin [Frederic reported to Fontana]. The enormous vaulting [the walls were three feet thick] is covered with dust; the window is small. Outside the window there are orange trees, palms, and cypresses. Opposite the window stands my bed under a Moorish filigree rosette. Next to the bed there is an old square writing desk that I can scarcely use; on it a leaden candle stick (this is a great luxury here) with a candle. Bach, my scribblings, and old papers (not mine)—silence. One can yell . . . still silence.

So this was the room in which Frederic was going to live and compose—"the cell of some old monk," said Frederic, "who perhaps had more fire in his heart than I have."

The energetic Sand, who could cope with any situation, set out to make the place as comfortable as possible. Still, certain things were beyond her power. Contrary to what she had been told, winter did not spare Majorca: from December on, rain storms and snow isolated them for weeks from even the little town where they were getting their provisions. The narrow path and the roads were either completely washed out or were too slippery and dangerous for walking. Furthermore, to make life even more trying, they were often awakened at night by a weird and ghostly visitor.

At regular intervals, a half-demented old man with a shepherd's crook would come to knock on the cell doors of the monastery, calling out the names of monks who were no longer there. It had formerly been his duty to summon them for their rites. By coincidence, while knocking on Frederic's door he called the name of Nicolas. Frederic, in an agony of spirit, was reminded of his father, whom he had not seen for more than three years. In the morning, Frederic and Sand would find the old man in one of the corridors, where, after his "dutiful errand," he would fall asleep with a knife in one hand and a rosary in the other.

Then, too, Frederic was often kept awake by the screams of small birds who were attacked outside his window and torn to pieces by eagles and vultures from the mountains above the monastery. Only Sand's care saved him from nervous collapse.

Several well-known stories try to explain the meaning of some of the compositions dating from this period of Frederic's life. They refer to his *Preludes*, and particularly to the one nicknamed "Raindrop Prelude." According to one such story, George Sand and her son, while returning from an errand to Palma, were overtaken by a thunderstorm that almost prevented them from reaching home safely. Frederic, worried over them, calmed himself by playing and improvising at the piano which had arrived shortly before from Pleyel. When, soaked through and through, George Sand and Maurice entered his room, they found him at the piano as if he were hypnotized. He told them that he thought they were both dead, that he himself had drowned in a lake, and that icy drops of water were falling on his chest.

"That was the rain drumming on the roof," they said. "I did not hear it," he replied.

Several *Preludes* were supposed to have been inspired by this experience, two in particular—Numbers 6 and 15—because both have the same repeated notes in a regular rhythm, suggestive of the sound of raindrops.

Actually, during the whole time he was in Majorca, Frederic composed only one new piece, a *Mazurka* that he called the "Palman Mazurka." But he did work on and complete a large number of his important works, that had already been sketched or started in Paris before he left for the south. Among these were his *Preludes*, the *Ballade in F major*, his third *Scherzo*, and two *Nocturnes*. He also continued work on his *Sonata in B flat minor*.

After three months in Majorca, Frederic needed a change. The quiet and solitude he had craved began to irritate him. He slept badly, was plagued by nightmares, and had a fever off and on. The adventure, hazardous for his health, and too dear a price for a few happy weeks, was over. George Sand, Maurice, and Frederic started on their way back to France.

12

*H*AD Chopin been well they would have gone directly back to Paris, but already in Palma he had suffered a hemorrhage. He refused to remain there faced with the dismal prospect of treatment by the local doctors. And to stay would mean missing the scheduled departure of the boat for Barcelona.

In great anxiety, Frederic was carried aboard the cargo ship, to discover himself in close company with a herd of pigs on deck. His bleeding continued, and the stench and the screams of the animals filling the air of his cabin brought even George Sand to despair. When they arrived in Barcelona, Chopin was more dead than alive.

Fortunately Sand managed to summon a doctor from a French warship that happened to be in the harbor. After twenty-four hours the bleeding was finally stopped. And after another week's rest at a hotel in Barcelona, they finally arrived in Marseilles. There a physician, an old friend of George Sand, advised her to take Chopin to her home in Nohant instead of going to Paris.

Frederic longed to return to the city, to see his friends and

get back to his life in his old environment, but had to agree
that some country air would speed his recovery. He had been
hearing about Nohant, but this would be his first visit to the
large two-story house with its beautiful garden. George Sand
saw to it that everything was done to insure peace and comfort
for her ailing guest. After the terrible experiences in Majorca
she knew exactly what Chopin needed. There seemed to be no
problem that was too much for her, no personal sacrifice too
great; she was the most devoted person he had known in his
life, and probably no one understood Chopin as she did.

Gentle, cheerful, and charming when well, Chopin drives intimate friends to despair when he is ill [George Sand used to say].
There is no nobler, more delicate soul, there is no man more loyal
and faithful in daily relationships. No one can surpass him in wit
and gaiety; no one has a fuller or deeper understanding of his art.
But unfortunately no one ever had a temperament so uneven, an
imagination so deranged and gloomy, a sensitivity so easily
wounded, and emotional demands so impossible to satisfy. Nothing of this is his fault; it is all the fault of his illness.

Whether consciously or not, Sand created for him just the
kind of family atmosphere he craved. Having given up the idea
of marriage in, at least, the near future, he accepted her family
as his own. Of her two children he felt closer to Solange,
because she possessed some musical talent. He taught her the
piano, ordered music for her from Paris, played duets with her,
and even became her confidant.

Maurice was a few years older than his sister. He and Chopin
shared no common interest in music; still, when Frederic had
completely recovered his strength, he always included the boy
in his favorite parlor games. Nohant, and the long evenings
spent either indoors by the fireside in the large drawing room
or on the terrace facing the garden, reminded Frederic of the
Skarbeks' home at Zelazowa Wola, where he had spent many
happy summer months with his family and his closest friends.

At Nohant, Frederic introduced the game of *tableaux vivants* to his "new family." For the so-called theatricals he wrote short plots; however, these had to be further improvised by the actors in the manner of *commedia dell'arte*. They also played charades, which, like the *tableaux*, he accompanied with improvisations at the piano.

During this time at Nohant, George Sand kept a watchful eye on Frederic's health. She supervised his diet and took him in her carriage on drives through the countryside where he could breath the fragrance of the meadows and enjoy the vast panorama of fields that reminded him of Poland. He had to go to bed early and to sleep late in the morning. No one was permitted to disturb him until late in the afternoon just before dinnertime. Frederic enjoyed perfect working conditions provided for him by Sand—probably the only person who had the opportunity to observe his working habits.

Chopin's compositions sound spontaneous, almost as if they were improvised. His early critics held this against him, in fact. It is true that often a whole composition was born in his mind while he amused himself by improvising at the piano, or while he was taking a walk in the garden, or driving in a carriage through the fields. He would try to retain it until he could jot down the general idea on paper. But then began the desperate labor of bringing to light the image he had so far only in his mind.

[According to Sand] it was a succession of efforts, hesitations, and moments of impatience to recapture certain details of the theme he could hear. He agonized over trying to write it down, and his dismay at his inability to recapture it in what he thought was its original purity threw him into despair. He would lock himself up in his room for a whole day, pacing back and forth, breaking his pens, repeating or changing one bar many times,

Left: George Sand's château at Nohant, a village in central France

writing and erasing it, and beginning again the next day with an
infinite perseverance. He sometimes spent six weeks on one page,
only in the end to write it exactly as he had sketched it at the
first draft.

Once he was satisfied with a composition he felt the need of
sharing it with someone, and George Sand, with her natural
talent for listening, was his best audience. He trusted her
judgment, although he needed no one for practical advice. To
these summer months at Nohant belong the following compositions: *Sonata in B flat minor* (Opus 35), which uses the
Funeral March written long before; the *Impromptu in F sharp
minor* (Opus 36); the *Two Nocturnes* (Opus 37); and the
third *Scherzo in C sharp minor* (Opus 39).

But the summer was drawing to a close, George Sand's
various visitors were departing, and Chopin also was thinking
of returning to Paris. He felt better, or at least as well as could
be expected. He wrote to his friend Fontana asking him to
look for two apartments: one for George Sand and one for
himself. He also asked him to begin decorating his new apartment, to try, if he could, to make it resemble his former home
as much as possible. Fontana was also to order hats, trousers,
shirts, and a black velvet vest for him from the most exclusive
men's shops. Frederic finished his letter in a rather jovial mood:
"Since you are so efficient, see to it that in my new apartment
no black thoughts or choking coughs come to me."

Upon his arrival in Paris, he moved in at 5 rue Tronchet;
George Sand was nearby at 16 rue Pigalle. But he complained
that his apartment was damp and dark, and he preferred Sand's
quarters, two pavilions in a walled-in garden. She and Solange
occupied the one with two large drawing rooms, while Maurice
lived in the other. Whenever he was free from his social obligations or lessons, Frederic spent most of the time at George
Sand's. Though he may have claimed her place was more

conducive to composing, Frederic actually hated the distance between their two homes; it separated him from the family life he craved. Finally, in the fall of 1841, still keeping his own apartment, Frederic moved to the rue Pigalle to share one of the pavilions with Maurice.

Life in each of these two pavilions had a distinctly different character: George Sand received her old friends—the writers, painters, poets and politicians—while Chopin received musicians and his old Polish friends. But this arrangement did not prevent them from occasionally joining each other on an evening with their guests. Even if he did not find much in common with some of Sand's friends and could not participate in literary or political discussions, Frederic was very happy about his new way of living in Paris. At these gatherings his presence was not overlooked, and sooner or later he was surrounded by an appreciative audience as he played the piano.

And there was one more factor that contributed to Frederic's happiness at this time. His close friend Countess Potočka, after an unsuccessful attempt at reconciliation with her husband, had returned to Paris.

Many books written about Chopin have dismissed the importance of Countess Potočka in his life, and have centered his personal life on his relationship with George Sand. In fact, a legend has been created linking these two names romantically. To doubt or repudiate this legend would be sacrilege had sufficient reason not been recently discovered. Only after the Second World War—that is, more than one hundred years after they were written—some of Chopin's letters to Potočka were made available to the public. These make clear that if Chopin was sincere—and there is no reason to doubt him—he could have loved only one woman in his life, Delphine Potočka.

Chopin's own words speak for themselves. In a most frank discussion of his life and relationship with George Sand, which

COUNTESS DELPHINE POTOĊKA

reveals his feelings for her, he wrote to Potoċka: "Only you and Sand have had my heart, and you more than anyone else because you know and understand me as no one else does. I haven't opened my heart to her; she is a foreigner and would not understand me." In this last sentence lies the key to his true feelings. It reflects the whole make-up of Chopin's personality.

He was a proud nationalist, who, because of his loathing of Russian domination in Poland, sacrificed his close ties with his family. If he were ever to marry, he could marry only a Pole. To speak to his wife or his children in any language except Polish was inconceivable to him.

But in his relationship with George Sand, there were more than the national and language barriers. Although outwardly a man of the world, whose manners and behavior were equal to those of anyone in the Parisian salons, Chopin had deeply rooted ideas of morality imbued in him by his own middle-class family.

He may have accepted George Sand's reputation and what he could not help seeing and hearing at close range, but to think that it did not affect his feelings for her would be a great error. Delphine Potocka was a beauty and an aristocrat, George Sand was neither; in fact, to the oddly snobbish Chopin, some of her ways seemed common. What he could forgive Potocka, as if she were one of his own family, he would never forgive George Sand.

Chopin needed someone to whom he could "open himself." At one time it was Titus; later it was no one except Potocka. George Sand was fully aware that during the eight years of her close friendship with Chopin she never could penetrate his inner self. She admitted that she could not even guess what was going on in his mind, and even used his very words, saying that he remained a foreigner to her.

In a letter to Potocka Frederic wrote: "The other women in my life were either youthful dreams buried long ago or winds of passion that blew only for a short while." The dreams of his youth must have been Konstancya and Maria, and as for "the winds of passion," they were too insignificant to have been recorded. "When a great love overwhelms me, when passion seizes me, and temptations tear at me like dogs, I forget about the world—as I once did with you—and I am ready to give up everything for a woman, to sacrifice my life and my work. With other women it wasn't so, with them I never lost my head."

As if to prove this point he reminded Potocka that while seeing her constantly he composed very little. His relationship with Sand, however, did not interfere with his creativity. And finally, if George Sand was, as others have said, the only woman he ever loved, how did it happen that he did not dedicate a single composition to her? It was not so with Potočka.

At this time, in Paris, Frederic was as happy as he could be: he had his family life with George Sand and her children, and he had Delphine Potočka to whom he could "open his heart."

His life once more assumed a regular routine: he spent winters in Paris and summers at Nohant. After his stay in Majorca, his old friends were more eager than ever to have him at their parties and dinners, and pupils begged him for lessons. As much as he disliked public appearances he occasionally consented to make one, usually inviting either a singer then in vogue, or an instrumentalist, to assist him. But now his performance of his own works filled most of the program.

His health was neither better nor worse, except that several incidents played havoc with his peace of mind. During the second winter in his pavilion he heard of the death of his old teacher, Zywny. It reawakened memories of his youth and of his own family. Frederic realized that most probably he would never see them again. In 1844, he received the sad news that his father, at the age of seventy-two, had died.

He found some solace in having Jan Matuszynski, his old friend, staying with him in Paris. Doctor Matuszynski was presumably there to take care of Frederic's health, but Matuszynski himself was suffering from tuberculosis, far more advanced than Chopin's. At times both the doctor and patient had to stay in bed. When, at the end of the winter, Matuszynski died, Chopin could not bear to remain at the pavilion, and George Sand took him back to Nohant, where she received only those friends whom Frederic liked.

Among them was Eugène Delacroix, who gave Maurice lessons in painting, and Pauline Viardot, the singer, who came with her husband. Delacroix was a great lover of music, and

Chopin's drawing room, Square d'Orléans

admired Chopin. Frederic, on the other hand, did not particularly care for Delacroix's paintings, though he did enjoy their discussions of art in general. He felt far happier with Pauline Viardot, who, although only twenty years old, impressed him with her exceptionally beautiful soprano voice. He played for her, accompanied her singing, and must have been amused and pleased when she vocalized some melodies from his *Mazurkas*.

Upon their return to Paris in the fall of 1842, George Sand found two apartments for them in the small Square d'Orléans, a secluded place favored by artists. But Frederic was restless; he saw his close friends either dying or departing, as did Julian Fontana, who, after many unsuccessful years of trying to establish himself as a pianist in Paris, finally went to the United States, as so many other Poles had done. With Fontana's departure he lost his most loyal lieutenant whom he had trusted, as a musician, with manuscripts to be copied and with discussions of business with publishers.

Not even the ideal atmosphere at Nohant could revive Frederic's spirits. George Sand saw no other solution than to write his mother suggesting that at least one member of his family should come to visit him. And indeed, on the arrival in Paris of Ludwika and her husband, Joseph Jedrzejevicz, it seemed to Frederic, who hastened to meet them, as if a beacon to a new life had suddenly appeared on a dark horizon.

Frederic put them up at George Sand's apartment and took great delight in showing them everything of interest in the city. He introduced them to his friends, took them to the opera and the theater, and spent hours listening to his guests' stories about everything dear to him in Poland. Then he took them to Nohant, where Sand greeted them with open arms. A woman of intelligence and tact, she knew when to leave them alone with Chopin, and when to entertain them with her utmost hospitality.

She won Ludwika's heart, and when, laden with gifts from Sand and Frederic to her mother and sister, Ludwika returned home, she found a letter from George Sand: "I assure you that you are the best physician he has ever had, because merely speaking to him about you is enough to restore to him his love for life."

Ludwika could only assure her mother that Frederic was well taken care of in his "adopted family."

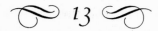

13

Bᴜᴛ Frederic's happiness in this adopted family did not last as long as everyone hoped. For years George Sand had carefully woven the threads of family relationships into a delicate fabric. Now it was threatening to disintegrate. This was caused not by anything that happened between Sand and Chopin, but by their attitudes toward the children.

Nothing really unusual was happening in Sand's family, but it is surprising that Chopin would allow himself to become involved. Too late, unfortunately, he found himself a "stranger."

It was one thing when in Majorca their "little Chopin"— he weighed less than one hundred pounds—went picnicking with the children, climbing mountains, telling fairy tales as they gathered flowers, or inventing games for them as if he were merely their elder brother, but quite another thing when Solange turned sixteen, developing the problems of a young and beautiful girl, and Maurice at twenty-one felt he had the right to assert his position as the man in the family, vacated by his father, who had divorced his mother years before.

Constant quarrels, most of them utterly trivial, between the children divided the four of them into two hostile camps.

George Sand loved Maurice more than her daughter, and always sided with him, while Solange turned to Chopin for support. This he readily gave her, for he preferred her to Maurice, who, he felt, was growing into an ill-mannered and presumptuous young man.

Of course, Chopin was foolish to take Maurice's displays of disrespect very seriously. And things he should have laughed at he took to heart. As an example of the triviality of their arguments it is enough to mention an occasion at dinner when Maurice helped himself to a breast of chicken and left a drumstick for Frederic, whereupon Chopin declared that he would never consent to being treated as an object of charity. Nor should he have paid any attention to the ridiculous gossip about his intentions of eventually marrying Solange.

The worst of it was that Chopin, constantly disturbed and irritated by what he called "civil war" in the family, no longer had the peace of mind for his own work. He took part less and less in the family's excursions, picnics, and his favorite theatricals. He felt that they did not enjoy his company. He withdrew into his own room, where he played the piano little and composed even less. He felt an outsider at Nohant. And there was no one to whom he could open himself, in whom he could confide everything that concerned and depressed him night and day. His only solace was writing letters to his family, sometimes two thousand words long, that now assumed the aspect of a diary.

In November, 1846, he was happy to return alone to Paris. Sand and her children remained in Nohant. Although he never went there again, this was not the end of his relationship with his adopted family, nor with George Sand. He should have, but did not, let the distance which separated them free him from further involvement in Sand's family business. He corresponded with her, and always showed the same sympathy and attention to Solange whenever she wrote to him.

At this time George Sand was already making decisive arrangements for the future of her children. She encouraged Maurice in his affection for a pretty, distant cousin, and she found two suitors for Solange among her visitors.

Where both her children were involved, George Sand invariably took their side against Chopin, so much so that he asked her finally whether she no longer cared for him. A silence fell between them, but Frederic could not accept it as a sign of the final breakdown in their relationship. He could not tear away from his attachment to her. He needed time.

Chopin was indifferent to her choice of Maurice's future wife, but was violently opposed to her schemes in regard to Solange. He had met both men: Louis Blanc, the famous socialist, who, in his opinion, would have been more interested in marrying Sand than her daughter; and Pierre Leroux, the poet, for whom Solange could not care in the least. Nor did Chopin congratulate her on her third choice—Fernand Préaulx, a local nobleman, their neighbor, whose engagement to Solange George Sand finally announced to him.

Perhaps even these common, purely family tribulations would have left no scars on the Sand-Chopin relationship, had Solange ultimately married Préaulx. Three months later, when George Sand and her family, including the fiancé, arrived in Paris to prepare Solange's trousseau and make the final arrangements for the wedding ceremony, Chopin resumed contact with them as if nothing had happened. Apparently he had accepted Préaulx at last. But Solange met Jean Clésinger, a young sculptor, fell in love with him, and broke her engagement.

Her mother accepted Solange's change of heart, but Chopin was furious. He did not like anything about the man: neither his overbearing physical appearance, nor his "vulgar manner"; nor did he have any respect for his work or his "presumed talent." Frederic predicted the worst calamity for Solange's future. But at this point George Sand had had enough of his advice. Solange married Clésinger.

Shortly after their honeymoon, however, Frederic's predictions came true. After a free-for-all squabble at Nohant—during which Clésinger attacked Maurice, and Maurice in return threatened to shoot him—Sand, trying to separate the two, was struck by her son-in-law. She turned the newlyweds out of her house.

Reporting to Chopin, Solange asked him a favor—the loan of his carriage at Nohant and some financial help. Frederic again came to her assistance. And this was the last straw for George Sand. She never forgave him. "He had no right to mix himself in my family business. It endangered the dignity and respect in my children's relations with me, their mother," she said.

Needless to say, Chopin did not take this final break easily, especially since he learned from their mutual friends that Sand had deliberately misunderstood his intentions and misrepresented the facts. "Sometimes she does not speak the truth," he said, "but this is permissible in a novelist." Several of their friends wrote to Sand, trying to make her see the injustice of her accusations against Chopin. Some of them even broke off their friendship with her. But Sand remained adamant. She stayed away from Paris, and only through her friends inquired about Chopin's health.

Frederic was not well. The long-drawn-out episode had taxed his nerves and his strength. He was consumed by a desperate loneliness. Most of his close friends were away from Paris: the musicians on their concert tours, Fontana in the United States. Out of old habit he ventured occasionally into "society," to the homes of the de Rothschilds and of Polish aristocrats. But they were strangers: he needed someone close to him. And Countess Potocka was in Nice recuperating from a severe illness.

FREDERIC CHOPIN, 1848
(*Portrait by Anton Kolberg*)

George Sand and Chopin did meet again. After spending an evening with a mutual friend and neighbor, Frederic was about to leave when, in the doorway, he encountered Sand who was arriving late at the party. As he greeted her, Sand felt his cold, trembling hand. He asked her if she had heard lately from Solange. "A week ago," Sand replied. Unaware of the reason for his question she resented his mention of her daughter as the first words he addressed to her after two years of separation.

"Solange has a daughter, and I am pleased to be the first to give you the news," Chopin said, bowed, and started down the stairs. Then he suddenly realized he had not told her that Solange was feeling well. He asked a friend who was with him to go back and tell Sand about her daughter; climbing the stairs again would have been a great effort for him.

George Sand came down and asked Chopin about Solange, and whether her husband was with her. Only then did she inquire about how he was himself.

"Very well," said Chopin.

There was nothing else they could say to each other. Frederic bowed again and walked out of the house.

"Was it my turn to ask him whether or not he still cared for me?" George Sand thought whenever she remembered the scene. She could still see the door of the house closing after him.

They never saw each other again.

⟡ 14 ⟡

*T*HE Revolution of 1848, which broke out in several central European countries, affected Chopin as it did most of his Polish friends in exile. Two years earlier they had heard of the unrest growing in their country, and now the news of a new revolt in several parts of Poland reawakened their hope for a free Poland, free at last from Russian rule. Again as it had happened in Vienna when he saw Titus hurry back home to join the Polish patriots in their fight against Russia, Frederic watched groups of political refugees embark for Poland on trains provided them by the French Government, which sympathized with their cause.

Seeing his friends off at the station, Chopin would say: "My public activity is over. If you have a little church in your village, give me a piece of bread, and in return I'll play for you in honor of the Holy Virgin." At this time when, because of his personal "drama," he felt completely dejected, desperately lonely, ill and incapable of working, the news of revolution revived his spirits.

To Julian Fontana in the United States he sent detailed reports of the progress his compatriots were making in Poland,

JANE STIRLING
(*Lithograph by Deveria*)

but he urged caution. "Let us not expend strength in vain, for strength is needed at the right moment. This moment is close, but it is not today. Perhaps in a month, perhaps in a year."

Meanwhile, disturbed by constant demonstrations and even street fighting in Paris, many of his friends were leaving the city. There could be no question of giving concerts or even lessons, and Chopin closed his apartment and went to London, where the musical season was in full swing. There his main financial support and advice on the management of his personal affairs came from Miss Jane Stirling, a former pupil. She belonged to a well-known Scottish family, and through her connections was chiefly responsible for the welcome Chopin received in the best London society. She and her sister, Mrs. Erskine, led him into a feverish life of perpetual social engagements.

During his three-month stay in London, Chopin played twice in public and three times at the homes of British nobility. His appearances were considered great events in the musical world, but he could barely enjoy his success. The climate and the weather were bad for him; he suffered frequent attacks of his illness and spent few days free from serious coughing and chills.

It was very difficult for Chopin to bear with all the visits, dinners, and soirees. They exhausted him. He thought he was suffering from some kind of nostalgia; he could not explain what it was, but he just did not know what to do with himself, and as he said, he could no longer be sad or glad, his feelings had dried up completely, and he was merely vegetating and waiting . . . waiting for what? He did not know himself.

Chopin was desperate and lonely, though he was never left alone. Even when he happened to have an evening free of social obligations Miss Stirling and her sister insisted on his dining with them. They were extremely kind ladies, but rather dull; yet he could not be rude and appear anything except very grateful for their attentions.

When the London musical season came to an end in July, Chopin could not return to Paris. He still had to journey to Scotland, to the home of his "two Scottish ladies." His stay there was a replica of that in London. He was taken to even more magnificent estates and castles than he had already seen. Soon he became saturated with all their splendor and the lavish hospitality of his hosts. Not knowing the language well enough to enjoy his admirers' discussions, he was bored by their conversations.

There are many ladies of all sorts here, aged lords in their seventies or eighties, and no young people at all, because they are out hunting [he reported in his letter home]. Here it is nothing but cousins of great families and great names that nobody on the Continent has ever heard of. The entire conversation turns about genealogy; it's like the Gospels—this one begat that one, and then that one begat, and again that one begat, and so on for two pages.

When he first decided to go to England he had hoped to start a new life there, but now after several months he realized that there was not much life left in him. His health was getting worse. Rains, dampness, and icy winds kept him in terror of catching cold, kept him indoors in large homes or castles where he could not find a room in which to be alone. "I am always surrounded by people, and I am alone, alone, alone."

Chopin could not adjust himself to the English way of living: "Today is Sunday," he explained in a letter to a friend. "No mail, no trains, no carriage (not even for a drive), nor any boat, nor even a dog to whistle to." His two Scottish ladies practically never left his side; they did everything they could think of to make him comfortable, to keep him entertained. And it was always the same from one month to the next. "They would have me stay and knock about the Scottish palaces. They are good-natured but so boring that God help me . . . and in the meantime, what has become of my art?" he wrote to a friend since there was no one there to confide in. "And where have I wasted my heart? I can scarcely recall how they sing in Poland. The world somehow passes me by. I forget, I have no strength. If I raise myself a little, I fall all the lower."

Upon his return to London his health worsened—he was in bed with a chill, headache, and choking—"all my bad symptoms," he said. Yet, he managed to appear at a concert for the benefit of Polish exiles. This was the last time he played in public.

A few days later, on the advice of his doctor, Chopin returned to Paris and somehow revived in the company of his old friends. Potočka was there, to his great happiness, and she often sang at his home, at the musical evenings he had resumed. He passed the winter months doing little teaching or composing. He wrote only two *Mazurkas*, his last compositions.

In the spring, an epidemic of cholera broke out in Paris. Chopin, so ill himself, was shocked by the death of many whom he knew, and some of his friends were again fleeing the city. He remained at his apartment only until another lodging was found for him at 74, Grande Rue, Chaillot, on the outskirts of Paris.

"I haven't begun to play," he told his friends. "I can't compose, and I don't know how I'll be living shortly." He was worried over his financial situation. The little money he brought from his trip to London had been spent already, and his health would not permit him to give any lessons. Fortunately, his friends came to his assistance, so that he did not have to depend entirely on selling his possessions.

Frederic could no longer conceal from his family the true state of his health and finances. Perhaps he knew that he was not going to live much longer. He wrote Ludwika begging her to come—to borrow money if necessary, but to come to see him. He said that when he recovered he could easily pay the debts, but she must come because, as all his friends would tell her, she was his best physician and best medicine. And then, as if he were confiding his most cherished dreams, he wrote: ". . . who knows? . . . perhaps I will go back to Poland with you—how we would all embrace each other then. . . ."

On the terrace of his apartment with a superb view of Paris, Frederic remained every day, lying on a chaise longue, waiting . . . waiting for the return of his strength, for his friends' daily visits, and the letters from Potočka who had gone again to Nice.

Ludwika arrived in July, and with her help Chopin moved, in late September, to another apartment—this time to 12, Place Vendôme, right in the heart of Paris. Although he was a dying man, he was genuinely interested in the arrangement of the furniture, which was brought to the apartment at his orders. But two weeks later even he accepted the fact that his days were numbered. Not a religious man, but for the sake of his mother, he asked for a priest to administer the last rites.

When Potočka heard that his end was near, she hurried back to Paris. "It was to enable me to see you that God has postponed calling me to Him," Frederic said when he saw her. Dressed in white, Potočka looked as beautiful as ever. Chopin asked her to sing for him, and his grand piano was rolled into his bedroom. She sang Stradella's "Hymn to the Virgin" and Marcello's "Psalm."

"The unhappy Countess, mastering her grief and suppressing her sobs, forced herself to sing," reported a friend who was there. "As for myself, I did not hear anything. I don't know what she sang. The whole scene, its contrasts, its intense sadness—all this was more than I could bear. I recall only the moment when Chopin's deadly coughing interrupted her second song."

Less than two days later, on October 17, 1849, at two in the morning Chopin died. He was only thirty-nine.

Chopin on his deathbed (*Drawing by Teofil Kwiatkovski*)

Appendix

ACCORDING to Robert Schumann, who claimed that he heard this from Chopin himself, the four *Ballades* were inspired by poems of the Polish poet Adam Mickiewicz. To my knowledge, these are the only works Chopin based on literary sources, but since it was the patriotic spirit rather than the subject of the poems that fired his imagination, one should not look for a programmatic "transcription" of Mickiewicz' words in musical terms.

The first *Ballade* was inspired by *Conrad Wallenrod*, an epic poem which retells a legend originated in Lithuania. At a banquet, Wallenrod praises the Moors who vengefully contaminated the Spaniards with pest, leprosy, and other horrible diseases which they had first voluntarily contracted. Wallenrod, a Pole, proclaims himself ready to do the same, to contaminate the oppressors of his country.

The second *Ballade* was based on a poem, translated roughly as "The Lake of the Willis (or nymphs)," which describes the site of a village once decimated by the Russians. To escape the dishonor of being delivered to the conquerors, the young women of the village pray to be engulfed by the earth. In answer to their prayer, they are turned into mysterious flowers growing around a lake. Their petals hold a curse for all who touch them.

The third *Ballade* was based on a poem entitled "L'Ondine" (the Undine), which tells of a young man who swears to remain faithful to his sweetheart. She is doubtful of his promise, however, and to test him first disappears and then returns disguised as an undine, or water spirit. The young man soon falls in love with her, and for this, his unfaithfulness, he is punished. He must follow the undine into the depths of a lake, but is never permitted to reach her.

The fourth *Ballade* was inspired by "The Three Budrys," the story of three brothers who are sent by their father to distant lands in search of treasure. When the three of them do not return, even at the beginning of winter, their father assumes they have been killed in battle. But finally, during a snowstorm, the three Budrys come home, each bringing with him a beautiful wife.

Selected Discography*

ANDANTE SPIANATO AND GRANDE POLONAISE (OP. 22)
Rubinstein (*see also* Mazurkas and Polonaise-Fantaisie)
3-*Victor* LM-6109

BALLADES, 1, 2, 3, 4 (OP. 23, 38, 47, 52)
Rubinstein   *Victor* LM-2370   **LSC-2370**

CONCERTO NO. 1 IN E MINOR FOR PIANO (OP. 11)
Brailowsky, Ormandy, Philadelphia Orchestra
Columbia ML-5652   **MS-6252**
Rubinstein, Skrowaczewski, New Symphony, London
Victor LM-2575   **LSC-2575**

CONCERTO NO. 2 IN F MINOR FOR PIANO (OP. 21)
Istomin, Ormandy, Philadelphia Orchestra
Columbia ML-5494   **MS-6159**
Rubinstein, Wallenstein, Symphony of the Air
Victor LM-2265   **LSC-2265**

FANTASIA IN F MINOR (OP. 49)
Rubinstein   *Victor* LM-2277

* Stereo recordings are listed in boldface.

IMPROMPTUS (4)

Rubinstein (*see also* Piano Music)   6-*Victor LM-6802*

KRAKOWIAK CONCERTO RONDO FOR PIANO & ORCHESTRA (OP. 14)

Askenase, Van Otterloo, Haag Residentie Orchestra
    Deutsche Grammophon DGG 18605   138085

MAZURKAS

Horowitz (7)   *Victor LVT-1032*

Rubinstein (*see also* Andante spianato and Polonaise-Fantaisie)
    3-*Victor LM-6109*

NOCTURNES (20)

Rubinstein (*see also* Piano Music)   6-*Victor LM-6802*

PIANO MUSIC

Horowitz   2-*Victor LM-1137*   1707

Lipatti (*see also* Sonata No. 3)   *Columbia ML-4721*

Rubinstein (includes Impromptus, Nocturnes, Polonaises,
Preludes, Waltzes)   6-*Victor LM-6802*

POLONAISE-FANTAISIE (OP. 61)

Richter (also Ballade No. 4)
    Deutsche Grammophon DGG 18849   138849

Rubinstein (*see also* Mazurkas and Andante spianato)
    Victor LM-2049

POLONAISES

Rubinstein (*see also* Piano Music)   6-*Victor LM-6802*

PRELUDES

Rubinstein (*see also* Piano Music)   6-*Victor LM-6802*

RONDO IN C FOR TWO PIANOS (OP. 73)

Luboshutz and Nemenoff   *Evergreen 6076*   3076

SCHERZOS 1, 2, 3, 4 (OP. 20, 31, 39, 54)

Rubinstein   *Victor LM-2368*   **LSC-2368**

SONATA NO. 2 IN B FLAT MINOR FOR PIANO (OP. 35)
    Gilels (*see also* Sonata No. 3)   *Bruno 14060L*
    Rubinstein (*see also* Sonata No. 3)
                  Victor LD-2554   LDS-2554

SONATA NO. 3 IN B MINOR FOR PIANO (OP. 58)
    Lipatti (*see also* Piano Music)   *Columbia ML-4721*
    Rubinstein (*see also* Sonata No. 2)
                  Victor LD-2554   LDS-2554

WALTZES (15)
    Brailowsky (14)   *Columbia ML-5628   MS-6228*
    Cortot (14)   *Angel COLH-32*
    Lipatti (14)   *Columbia ML-4522*
    Rubinstein (*see also* Piano Music) *6-Victor LM-6802*

Index

PICTURE CREDITS